The EU's Limited Leverage

Normative Power vs. Gulf Realpolitik

GEW Social Sciences, With Hichem Karoui (Ed.)

Global East-West (London)

Copyright © 2025 by GEW Social Sciences

Editor: Hichem Karoui.

Collection: The Gulf. Global East-West (London).

All rights reserved.

No portion of this book may be reproduced in any form without written permission from the publisher or author, except as permitted by copyright law.

Contents

1. Foundations of the EU's Normative Power in Global Politics — 1
2. The Gulf Region — 13
3. EU-Gulf Relations — 25
4. Normative Power in Practice — 35
5. Gulf Realpolitik — 47
6. The Paradox of Dependence — 59
7. Case Study — 69
8. Case Study — 81
9. Challenges to EU's Normative Authority in the Gulf — 91
10. The Impact of Gulf Realpolitik on EU's Normative Goals — 103
11. Power Dynamics — 113
12. Practical Strategies For the EU to Enhance Normative Leverage — 125
13. Navigating the Tensions — 135

14. Future Outlook   147

15. Conclusion   159

References   171

1
Foundations of the EU's Normative Power in Global Politics

Defining the EU's Normative Power: Principles and Ambitions

The economic trajectories of Gulf nations have broadly been defined, of course, by their substantial oil and gas reserves. For quite some time, these resources have been the primary drivers behind swift modernisation, the generation of substantial wealth, and considerable regional power [1]. The consistent export of hydrocarbons onto the global stage provided substantial income, which in turn financed various infrastructure developments, social welfare initiatives, and different state-building operations. However, such a reliance on oil and gas has also resulted in specific vulnerabilities; namely, the potential for global price volatility to disrupt financial planning with surprising speed [2]. Moreover, the non-renewable nature inherent to fossil fuels inevitably prompts contemplation regarding extended sustainability.

The European Union is often regarded as a promoter of human rights, democracy, and multilateral cooperation—values that are at the very core of its normative power [3]. It aspires to shape global relations by advocating for these ideals, and frequently views itself as a moral leader on governance and social justice. This ambition is evident in the EU's diplomacy, treaties, and standards for trade agreements, as it strives for a world guided by tolerance and respect among nations. The EU's commitment to global governance is further demonstrated through its championing of international laws and its active participation in peacekeeping missions. However, the daily grind of global politics throws some serious curveballs.

For example, the EU faces a dilemma: balancing its normative agenda with economic interests, particularly regarding energy dependence on Gulf states. The need for stable energy supplies from the Gulf forces the EU to address regimes whose human rights records do not align with its proclaimed values. These contradictions really highlight the tug-of-war between principle and pragmatism in EU foreign policy. The EU sees itself as a symbol for optimism and a model for good governance. It aims to spread democracy, uphold human rights, and foster multilateralism in an increasingly polarised world [4].

Still, this vision often clashes with geopolitical realities. For instance, Germany's arms sales to Saudi Arabia—actions that go against the EU's own human rights standards—have triggered protests and debates both in Germany and across Europe, highlighting the complexities when economic or security interests bump heads with principles. Similarly, France's establishment of naval bases in the UAE illustrates the strategic calculations EU nations make, demonstrating a commitment to securing trade routes and regional stability. At the same time, it forces an uncomfortable realisation: such moves may prop up regimes at odds with the democratic values the EU seeks to promote. These instances show the persistent conflict between the EU's stated principles and its actual actions, creating a detailed debate about the legitimacy of its normative power. Understanding this tension is really crucial for analysts, policymakers, and anyone interested in the EU's global role. The EU's approach suggests that moral authority in international relations is fragile; engaging with autocratic regimes often raises questions about the sincerity and effectiveness of its normative power. Even though the EU strives to act on its values, the complexities of global politics necessitate a nuanced understanding and a willingness to adapt. For researchers and diplomats, keeping an eye on these dualities can significantly enhance our understanding of how global governance operates in practice, demonstrating that it is not just about ideals but also about the ongoing struggle to align actions with values in a world that is anything but predictable.

The historical evolution of EU foreign policy and moral authority

The EU's perceived moral high ground is deeply rooted in its very origins—a continent scarred significantly by two devastating global conflicts, striving for lasting peace through collaborative unity and a shared set of core values [5]. The visionary founders of European integration conceived a community based not only on economic considerations but, crucially, on a firm commitment to democratic governance, fundamental human rights, and the impartial rule of law. This aspiration positioned the EU as more than just a marketplace; it aspired to be a normative power, aiming to project its values alongside its implemented policies. However, this noble ideal has frequently contended with the complex realities of realpolitik. The EU's role in moral leadership was not simply given; rather, it emerged from a demanding crucible where idealistic principles met with the pragmatic pressures of politics, security considerations, and economic imperatives. While the EU presents itself as a champion of multilateral cooperation and human rights, its foreign policy choices often involve a subtle balancing act between the forceful advocacy of its core values and the careful management of essential relationships with diverse global partners. During the Cold War, Europe's ethical position was partly a response to stark ideological divisions but also a practical strategy for post-war reconstruction. The establishment of institutions promoting human dignity and international cooperation provided a significant contrast with authoritarian regimes elsewhere. This historical context is essential for comprehending the development of the EU's normative power and its reaction to global conflicts [6].

As time passed, the EU's ongoing enlargement and strengthened political ties solidified its claims to normative authority. However, this assertion has faced challenges both internally and externally. Member states have debated the potential costs of fully embracing human rights internationally, particularly when such commitments could jeopardise valuable economic prospects or key strategic alliances. This tension is particularly evident in relations with the Gulf states, where economic interests, especially energy security, have complicated the EU's ability to assert moral leadership without being perceived as making compromises. The EU inspires by providing a model for peaceful collaboration, which starkly contrasts with traditional powers that often rely on military strength in their diplomatic approaches. However, the EU's inherent idealism is tempered by the practical considerations of its member states' varied interests, which influence its decision-making processes and occasionally restrict its capacity to act with a unified moral voice. It remains a force promoting core values, but it is also wary of endangering its geopolitical standing and economic stability. The evolution of EU foreign policy reflects an ongoing interplay between aspirational goals and the unavoidable demands of global politics.

Over the decades, Brussels has strived to develop a foreign policy that closely reflects the principles enshrined in its founding treaties—namely, human rights, democracy promotion, and conflict prevention. However, in the face of real-world situations, these goals often encounter considerable friction. The Gulf region provides a notable example of this tension. Officially, the EU champions democracy and human rights. However, Gulf states remain essential energy suppliers and key strategic partners, frequently exhibiting political systems that do not necessarily align with European democratic ideals. This dynamic creates a tightrope walk for Brussels: maintaining dependable energy sources while simultaneously advocating for reforms or improvements in governance and human rights records. Case studies provide further insight into this intricate balance. Germany's continued arms sales to Saudi Arabia, generally speaking, highlight the pragmatic aspects of EU foreign policy. Despite widely shared concerns regarding Riyadh's involvement in the Yemen conflict and its less-than-ideal human rights record, German industry and political circles justify these sales on both economic and strategic grounds. This pragmatism contrasts with the European Union's stated intention to promote peace and human rights, revealing inconsistencies within the organisation. Conversely, France's naval base in the United Arab Emirates rather exemplifies a pragmatic approach to its security and broader regional influence. France uses its military presence to project power and protect its interests while navigating the complex political landscape of the Gulf, sometimes compromising its normative aspirations when they conflict with its primary strategic objectives.

Introduction to EU Foreign Policy

The EU's foreign policy demonstrates a frequent swing between its ideals and the demands of global politics. At times, the combined voice of the Union struggles against the specific aims of its members, especially when those members possess different connections or investments in the Gulf region. Given that energy security remains a core concern, the EU's desire to promote multilateralism and human rights can clash with its need for partners whose actions do not always align with these values. As a result, EU foreign policy can appear contradictory, with moral principles presented alongside—and sometimes undermined by—practical considerations. Comprehending this inherent tension helps explain the difficulties the EU faces as it attempts to establish a clear role in international affairs. This situation poses a challenge for diplomats, policymakers, and academics, as it forces them to acknowledge the disparity between what the EU aims to achieve and its actual outcomes. The EU aims to be a power driven by norms.

However, its dependence on Gulf energy and the complex political situation in the area require compromises, a reality highlighted by the fact that norms guide EU actions but are often secondary to its interests in situations like Ukraine [7]. Such an arrangement complicates the Union's efforts and attracts criticism from those who see its position as hypocritical and from partners who doubt the honesty of its promises. Dealing with this complexity requires nuanced policies and a willingness to make tough choices between values and interests. A key question is how the EU could improve its foreign policy consistency by better aligning its internal beliefs with its external partnerships. Open decision-making processes and honest discussions about these tensions could foster greater trust among citizens and allies. Only then can the EU present a more consistent and believable image that aligns with the complex world it is trying to influence, supporting the idea that even with closer defence cooperation, it is primarily strengthening its position as a civilian power on the global stage [8].

Theoretical Frameworks: Soft Power, Normative Power, and Power Projection

Soft power offers a route to influence, not via coercion, but by shaping how others perceive the world and what they desire; the EU has used it extensively in its foreign policy. The Union has historically used its culture, core values, and appealing ideas to attract other nations. Consider the EU's promotion of democracy, human rights, or environmental rules—it hopes that others will embrace these, not because they face pressure, but because these concepts resonate with them [9]. Soft power requires patience, subtly introducing ideas and fostering trust, leading to eventual cooperation without any apparent force. Think of it as carefully planting seeds, hoping for growth over time—frequently more successful than relying on threats or penalties. Normative power expands on this, suggesting that influence stems from deeply shared ethics and beliefs.

The EU's capacity to define international benchmarks, then, is not simply about its economic muscle; it also involves setting moral examples that others hope to emulate [10]. The EU positions itself as a symbol of ethical leadership by championing multilateralism and human rights, attracting others who see genuine value in its approach. Nevertheless, using normative power is not always simple, given that some critics contend that the EU can struggle to meet the high standards it sets for itself, especially when financial considerations become paramount. Still, normative power, at its core, aims to craft international norms by focusing on ethics, justice, and equity. Power projection, by contrast, encompasses more explicit methods in which a country or union demonstrates its strength globally. It often involves military resources, strategic positioning, or political influence that can shape events or deter challengers. The EU's strategy here tends to be more nuanced, opting for alliances, diplomatic actions, or limited military aid instead of deploying robust power. For instance, Germany might supply arms to Saudi Arabia, seeking to affect regional power balances, or France could keep naval facilities in the Gulf region to protect its interests.

The Complexities of Power Projection in the EU's Global Strategy

Sometimes, actions—although potentially clashing with the EU's stated ethical principles—represent a type of power projection that complements softer methods. This underscores the inherent struggle between the ideal and the real, particularly when economic or security needs conflict with normative commitments [11]. In practice, these frameworks often interconnect. To illustrate, EU initiatives aimed at promoting human rights rely on soft power and a strong moral position. However, behind the scenes, strategic diplomatic manoeuvres and military alliances—reflecting aspects of power projection—are also employed [12]. Maintaining equilibrium among these strategies can prove precarious. For instance, some may perceive Germany's arms sales as a threat to its peace reputation, leading to criticism. Conversely, France's naval presence serves multiple strategic objectives. This blend of methods highlights the difficulties in applying related theories to actual geopolitics, a domain where ideals often face trials from urgent interests and evolving alliances. Comprehending these frameworks helps clarify the EU's persistent issue: how can influence be projected without compromising moral authority?

In general, advocating for human rights or multilateralism proves simpler verbally than in practice, especially when energy security or economic links with nations in the Gulf region necessitate pragmatic compromises. The EU might waver in its attempts to enforce norms against arms exports to regimes allegedly involved in rights violations when energy imports from those nations become crucial. This discrepancy underscores the importance of recognising the distinctions and overlaps among soft power, normative power, and power projection—each of which influences the EU's global role in diverse and sometimes conflicting ways. Recognising the practical operations of these approaches can assist policymakers in creating more cohesive strategies. Practically, bolstering soft power could involve increasing cultural exchanges or supporting civil society initiatives, whereas mitigating the effects of power projection might entail transparent diplomacy or multilateral agreements. These combined tactics, when thoughtfully applied, may provide the EU a more consistent global voice, thus aligning its actions more harmoniously with its espoused principles. One tangible measure could involve incrementally decreasing arms sales to questionable governments while boosting diplomatic participation, therefore converting firm power into a complement to—rather than a contradiction of—soft influence.

2
The Gulf Region
Geopolitical Landscape and Strategic Significance

The Gulf Region: Geopolitical Landscape and Strategic Significance

The European Union's desire to promote its values—such as human rights and multilateral cooperation—frequently encounters issues, often linked to its dependence on energy imports from the Gulf. Specifically, the extensive oil reserves and natural gas deposits held by Gulf Cooperation Council states have become essentially vital for Europe's economy; however, this makes it harder for the EU to stand firm on its principles. The issue is that moral positions become somewhat muddled when discussions about democratic reforms or human rights abuses arise, and economic interests also come into play. It creates a bit of a shadow. This impacts the EU's normative clout, complicating advocacy for its values without seeming inconsistent. Take, for example, Germany's continued arms sales to Riyadh [12] – a point of international concern given the situation in Yemen. This highlights a certain contradiction, where the EU supports conflict prevention and democracy, yet material support through weapons somewhat weakens its position. Similarly, France's military presence, with naval bases in the United Arab Emirates, shows yet another facet of this complex dynamic [13].

While French forces stationed there ostensibly ensure stability, benefiting both sides, it also inevitably aligns France more closely with the Gulf states than perhaps an entirely principled actor might be. The EU, a diverse group, faces the challenge of balancing these factors. As a result, its approach may seem hesitant, reducing its ability to effect change. It underscores how critical energy ties can be but simultaneously act as a restriction, undermining its voice even as it provides leverage. Looking ahead, for the EU to broaden its influence beyond these dependencies, it needs stronger relationships that extend beyond energy. Consider alliances formed around shared objectives in areas such as technology, education, health, and climate policy. Encouraging collaboration in these areas, as well as on alternative energy and diversification projects, could reduce those risky dependencies. There is so much potential beyond oil and pipelines – for joint research, cultural exchange, and private sector links – that could forge constructive connections.

Historical Context and Political Structures of Gulf States

The Gulf region presents a compelling blend of history and culture, one where old ways meet new developments [14]. Initially, governance took shape in fishing and pearl-diving villages, typically under the leadership of tribal chiefs who held considerable local power. These tribal systems functioned through alliances, managing relationships and conflicts in a manner that shaped governance—an approach that persisted even as trade grew. The 20th-century oil boom, however, brought about significant changes. It brought rapid wealth to some states, altering their politics and society. Nations such as Saudi Arabia and the UAE quickly moved from tribal systems to modern states, often centralising power to handle resources effectively. Regional geopolitics has long been influenced by external factors, particularly British colonial involvement, which shaped the formation of these states' political identities. Protectorate treaties solidified British influence and reduced local disputes, thereby integrating a colonial past into the area's ongoing political story [15].

Gulf States' Political Landscape and Global Alliances

The wave of decolonisation during World War II thrust Gulf states into a world where they had to manage their own sovereignty amidst changing power balances. Their strategic geography unexpectedly made them key players in regional and global politics, leading to various security pacts and political allegiances, particularly during the Cold War. Leaders had to balance traditional tribal duties with modern state needs, which often complicated internal affairs [16]. Generally speaking, governance in the Gulf often leans towards monarchies, each with its own power structure. Saudi Arabia, for example, has a royal family that is deeply woven into governance and Islamic faith, providing legitimacy but potentially limiting political participation. However, countries like Qatar and Kuwait, which are also monarchies, have parliamentary systems that provide some public representation. This mix of monarchic traditions and new political institutions highlights the region's governance complexities. Tribal loyalties continue to shape political realities, as leaders still rely on tribal support for legitimacy, indicating how traditional practices persist even in modern governance [17].

Personal connections and family ties often matter more than institutional affiliations in decision-making, hindering the development of robust civil societies where citizens might prioritise loyalty to family or tribal leaders over the state. Despite modernisation efforts, many Gulf states remain tied to historical practices that challenge the full realisation of democratic norms. The relationship between Gulf states and the European Union brings up tough questions about human rights and multilateralism. For example, Germany's arms sales to Saudi Arabia demonstrate a pragmatic approach to foreign relations, striking a balance between strategic interests and ethical considerations. Critics argue that dealing with regimes known for human rights abuses undermines European values. Likewise, France's military cooperation with the UAE—such as establishing naval bases—raises questions about how a military presence affects regional stability and democratisation. The situation in Gulf states presents both opportunities and challenges for outside powers, so understanding their history, political structures, and relationships with global powers is essential for navigating their complex political landscape effectively. Observers and policymakers should consider these factors when handling economic and diplomatic relations with Gulf nations, while upholding a commitment to human rights and governance. A practical approach may involve recognising their historical context, acknowledging the intersections of tradition and modern governance that shape their societies today.

Table (1): Gulf States' Political Landscape and Global Alliances

Country	Political System	Key Alliances	Regional Influence
Saudi Arabia	Absolute Monarchy	United States,China,OPEC+	High
United Arab Emirates	Federal Absolute Monarchy	United States,China,OPEC+	High
Qatar	Absolute Monarchy	United States,Turkey,GCC	Moderate
Kuwait	Constitutional Monarchy	United States,GCC	Moderate
Oman	Absolute Monarchy	United States,GCC	Moderate
Bahrain	Constitutional Monarchy	United States,GCC	Moderate

Gulf States' Political Landscape and Global Alliances

Economic Foundations: Oil, Gas, and Diversification Efforts

The economic stories of the Gulf states are intertwined mainly with their substantial oil and gas resources, which are central to transforming relatively small economies into significant actors on the world stage. These resources have, for many years, driven quick modernisation, a build-up of wealth, and amplified regional influence. Hydrocarbon flows to global markets generated substantial income, which then supported crucial infrastructure developments, social welfare initiatives, and nation-building activities, demonstrating the importance of energy exports to national advancement [18]. Still, this reliance on oil and gas has exposed vulnerabilities, increasingly evident now. Global market price volatility disrupts financial plans rapidly, creating issues related to economic stability. Furthermore, the finite nature of fossil fuels has raised serious questions about long-term sustainability, prompting discussions about the need for economic diversification and the adoption of renewable energy alternatives [19]. So, while the narrative of the Gulf's economic growth definitely shows notable progress and change, it also highlights the dangers associated with relying too heavily on hydrocarbon resources.

Table (2): **EU Energy Import Dependency and Diversification Efforts**

Country	Energy Import Dependency Ratio (%)	Diversification Index
Austria	0.223	0.7663
Belgium	0.578	0.7977
Bulgaria	0.6443	-1.1097
Croatia	-0.3932	1.1599
Cyprus	0.5389	0.916
Czech Republic	0.3556	-1.7785
Denmark	-3.9348	0.6915
Estonia	-1.0641	-1.5009
Finland	0.7418	0.0879
France	0.457	0.7567
Germany	0.3478	-0.424
Greece	0.2737	-1.4212
Hungary	-0.128	-0.7862
Ireland	0.5077	0.2496
Italy	0.1372	0.8243
Latvia	0.5155	0.6456
Lithuania	0.2347	0.9088
Luxembourg	0.5116	0.916
Malta	0.6794	-1.4985
Netherlands	0.2932	1.1961
Poland	0.1606	-1.7496
Portugal	0.3907	0.805
Romania	-1.5673	-1.0421
Slovakia	0.0514	0.4476
Slovenia	0.3361	-1.03
Spain	0.3985	0.1989
Sweden	0.5585	0.4911
United Kingdom	-1.8481	0.4814

EU Energy Import Dependency and Diversification Efforts

Economic Diversification and Geopolitical Challenges in the Gulf

The Gulf countries continue to be vital on the global stage, their economies strongly linked to oil. To address this reliance, some have invested in areas such as refining, petrochemicals, and LNG. These help add value and buffer against raw material price volatility; yet, oil's role remains significant. Governments depend on oil and gas for most of their income, making them open to demand shifts or supply problems, which pose geopolitical issues, especially for Europe, a large energy consumer from the Gulf. The EU, while promoting human rights and cooperation, faces a challenge: needing Gulf energy while navigating complex relationships with its autocratic partners. Germany's arms deals with Saudi Arabia [20] show this, where strategy can outweigh values. France's establishment of naval bases in the UAE illustrates how energy and security often intersect, highlighting the Gulf's significance beyond its energy resources. Recognising these issues, Gulf nations have launched ambitious plans to diversify their economies, a significant undertaking, generally speaking. Decades of wealth have created government sectors and financial frameworks built around hydrocarbons, making profound change hard. Transitioning to knowledge-based economies necessitates the development of new industries, enhanced education, and the encouragement of entrepreneurship. This faces challenges, including nationalisation of the workforce and regional competition. However, there are opportunities in tech, renewable energy, tourism, and finance.

Nations such as the UAE and Saudi Arabia have outlined visions for sustainable growth and reduced oil dependence by expanding into non-oil sectors. While these plans have had successes, especially in attracting foreign businesses and fostering innovation, proper diversification is an ongoing process [21]. The journey toward economic change necessitates striking a balance between modern economic reforms and social norms. Subsidies, benefits, and job patterns linked to oil create resistance. Economic opening sometimes encounters caution due to the need to maintain social stability. Nevertheless, the push continues because oil supplies are finite, and the global move to green energy adds urgency. For Europe and the Gulf, this presents both opportunities and challenges for collaboration. The EU's green shift means gradually reducing fossil fuel use in the Gulf, compelling Gulf states to find alternative ways to grow more quickly. Still, their investment in renewables aligns with parts of Europe's sustainability vision. Navigating this will need dialogue, with diversification as a key to a balanced partnership between these regions. A practical approach for those looking at Gulf economies is to observe how energy export earnings are reinvested, both locally and abroad. Diversification success depends on investing oil profits not just in striking projects but also in education, smaller businesses, and infrastructure that support sustainable growth. Note how these leaders manage oil sector dominance versus new industries to gain insights into the region's economic future.

Security Dynamics and External Influences in the Gulf

The Gulf has traditionally presented a complex array of interwoven security challenges. Historically, external players have significantly contributed to shaping the political landscape and influencing regional stability in this region [Gulf International Forum, 2020]. Notably, Western powers, specifically those from Europe and North America, maintain strategic interests that significantly impact local security structures. These manifest through diplomatic efforts, military support, and economic relationships, which can both complicate and stabilise the region's security dynamics [Katzman, 2021]. The Gulf Cooperation Council (GCC), a regional alliance, serves as a buffer yet reflects the broader tensions between external powers and local ambitions [Shah, 2020]. This intricate network underscores that security considerations in the Gulf extend beyond local concerns, becoming a global arena where interests intersect and occasionally collide [Friedman, 2021]. External entities deliver both reassurance and potential danger; the U.S., for instance, maintains a robust military presence through bases in Bahrain, Qatar, and the UAE—strategic footholds that embody larger geopolitical aims [Carafano, 2021]. These, however, can also spark regional dissent, reminding us that external involvement cuts both ways [Mansoor, 2020]. Likewise, Europe plays a subtle yet consistent role through arms exports and diplomatic initiatives. Countries such as the UK and France strive to project influence, albeit avoiding confrontation [Wiessala, 2020].

Beyond military tactics, external powers also shape the security architecture through economic aid and policies, including counter-terrorism efforts, tech investments and intelligence sharing. These all create a complicated, rarely simple, security system [Sullivan, 2021]. While regional alliances offer a semblance of collective defence, they frequently showcase underlying tensions because Gulf countries have often leaned on external powers for defence while also competing amongst themselves [Rassler, 2020]. The Saudi Arabia-Qatar rivalry, for example, significantly shapes security policies, with each aiming to reinforce its regional influence through alliances. States such as Oman and Kuwait are inclined towards neutrality, acting as mediators inside the region rather than participants in disputes [Dorsey, 2021]. These dynamics within the region often deepen external powers' engagement, leading them to take sides based on their strategic calculations [Meyer, 2020].

The tensions involving Iran and the Gulf states further complicate matters, frequently drawing external players more deeply into local conflicts [Kamrava, 2021]. Consequently, the Gulf's security landscape presents a complex mix of conflict, coexistence, and external actions, delicately balanced by influences and interests. Within this complex setting, the EU has its own issues. It advocates for multilateralism, human rights, and democracy, but these beliefs frequently clash with the practical realities of Gulf politics [Cameron, 2020].

Given its reliance on Gulf energy resources, particularly oil and gas, the EU hesitates to confront authoritarian regimes harshly or reconsider its strategic alliances [Cameron, 2020]. Germany's significant arms exports to Riyadh, for example, proceed despite critiques of the kingdom's internal policies and human rights record. This generates a diplomatic challenge: balancing the promotion of ethics with ensuring energy security through trade [Smith, 2021]. France highlights another aspect through its naval facilities in the UAE, framed as stability-focused partnerships, while also symbolising broader strategic interests [Le Monde Diplomatique, 2020]. The EU must navigate a precarious path between advocating human rights and reform and preserving vital security and energy ties. This task is notably challenging when moral principles, regional stability requirements, and energy market demands appear to be heading in different directions [Allison, 2021].

Local Security and Diplomatic Perspectives

Local security dynamics can highlight areas of concern, be they potential flashpoints or zones of relative calm [24]. Regarding energy policy, the decision to rely on Gulf oil entails specific strategic considerations [25]. Reducing dependence on potentially unstable regions can be achieved through diversification of energy sources or by investing in renewable technologies. Diplomacy-wise, transparent engagement with Gulf states about human rights, alongside support for security initiatives in the region, might allow for more well-rounded relationships to develop. Observing shifts in external power strategy—such as changes in military deployments, intelligence cooperation, or economic engagement—can hint at future stability, or otherwise. The Gulf, it seems, is a complex arena of competing interests, where every action has global reverberations—keeping up to date with these evolving dynamics aids in understanding the overall security landscape in an increasingly connected world.

3
EU-Gulf Relations
A Historical Overview

EU-Gulf relations have evolved as a complex interaction between the EU's aspirations and the realities of Gulf politics. At first, the EU was mostly interested in economics because it wanted to become a major trade partner in a region rich in energy. This was especially true after the 1973 oil crisis, which made the Gulf states more important. This economic base set the stage for subsequent political talks, which were formalised in the 1989 EU-GCC Cooperation Agreement. The design of this agreement was to establish a comprehensive partnership that encompassed security, trade, and cultural connections.

However, the EU's goal of being a normative power—based on promoting democracy, human rights, and the rule of law—often clashed with the way many Gulf Cooperation Council (GCC) states are governed, which are often authoritarian. The Arab Spring and its aftermath further complicated the situation. The EU had to balance its rhetoric about norms with the practical need to secure energy and maintain stability in a volatile region. As a result, while the EU has attempted to act as a normative force in the Gulf, its limited influence has been underscored by the ongoing priorities of Gulf states, highlighting the tension between idealism and pragmatic statecraft in international relations. In most cases, the complexities are a result of the EU's aspirations and realities on the ground.

Early Engagements and Diplomatic Foundations

The story of how the European Union (EU) and Gulf coun-

THE EU'S LIMITED LEVERAGE 27

tries got to know each other starts in the 1970s. It was a time when both sides realised they could benefit from each other in areas such as trade, securing energy supplies, and promoting regional stability (Khan, 2019). The EU, with its growing economies, really needed the oil that the Gulf region had (Smith, 2020). On the other hand, Gulf countries, which had abundant oil resources, sought to attract capital and new technologies from other countries, particularly those in Europe (Al-Muhanna, 2021). This need for each other marked the beginning of talks that would unfold over many years. From a broader perspective, the EU also sought to collaborate with the Gulf due to global developments. The issues of the Cold War led European leaders to recognise the need for allies outside their own regions (O'Sullivan, 2018). By forming alliances with Gulf countries, they gained more options for energy and had some protection if things became shaky in the Middle East (Jones, 2020). Those in charge recognised that, by fostering these relationships, they could collaborate more effectively on security issues, such as combating terrorism and maintaining maritime safety in the region (Rogers, 2022).

Initially, these talks involved important individuals visiting each other and initiating official conversations, which demonstrated their desire to collaborate (Baker, 2019). A big moment was when they signed the Cooperation Agreement in 1988. It was like setting the stage for future collaboration on both political and financial matters (Wilkins, 2021). This agreement enabled them to collaborate on various areas, including trade, technology, and even culture, thereby strengthening their connection (Green, 2022). Over time, some significant agreements have brought the EU and Gulf countries closer together. For instance, when Germany sold weapons to Saudi Arabia, it demonstrated that European countries were willing to engage in business, despite the EU occasionally having concerns about issues such as human rights (Müller, 2019).

Additionally, when France established naval bases in the UAE, it demonstrated its intention to collaborate on military matters while also safeguarding crucial trade routes (Lévy, 2020). These moves were crucial for framing the EU-Gulf connection around issues that both parties cared about, even if some moral complexities lay beneath. These initial steps demonstrated a clear shift in the situation. These talks marked the beginning of more organised partnerships in the years that followed, which ultimately altered the political landscape in both areas (Benson, 2021). The most important thing to remember from this time is the crucial importance of nurturing these relationships (Thompson, 2022).

Trade, Investment, and Energy Ties Over the Decades

The economic entanglement between the European Union and the Gulf states is about exchanging what each needs, a relationship that has been decades in the making. Energy, particularly oil and gas, has been a linchpin. European nations, you see, lean heavily on Gulf exports to keep their industries and homes running. As Gulf states grew richer from energy sales, Europe found itself increasingly reliant on those resources to sustain its economy [30]. This dependency? It has subtly shifted diplomatic priorities, often moving away from focusing solely on political issues or human rights and more on maintaining energy and expanding business

THE EU'S LIMITED LEVERAGE 29

opportunities. You have seen things like trade corridors popping up, investments in ports and pipelines, and joint ventures – all signs of this changing relationship and evolving power dynamics in the global economy. Economic interests have not only shaped ties but also, at times, reshaped the conversation between the EU and Gulf nations. Trade agreements that cut tariffs and smooth out trade have coexisted alongside those big energy deals, which offer stability but also come with their set of challenges. For Europe, securing its energy supply has meant collaborating with governments whose values and human rights records often diverge from European ideals. This tension? It is a consistent backdrop to talks where practical gains and ethical questions meet.

Sometimes, the drive to identify different energy sources has led European countries to tweak their policies in the Gulf's direction. It is a complex situation where oil and gas contracts can sometimes trump questions of democracy or free speech. Take Germany, for example. Its big arms deals with Saudi Arabia show how economic interests can sometimes overshadow those human rights commitments the EU champions [31]. Even with all the public concern about the Saudi-led mess in Yemen and the civilian casualties, German companies have kept supplying weapons to Riyadh. These sales really highlight the importance placed on economic and strategic ties, perhaps even more so than humanitarian principles.

The German government often claims that controlling these sales enables it to monitor the situation. Critics, though, argue that it is more of a wink and a nod to questionable behaviour in exchange for money and influence. This is a delicate balancing act. When big money and alliances are involved, it exposes the limitations of Europe's ethical objectives. Similarly, France's maintenance of naval bases in the United Arab Emirates reveals another aspect of this pragmatic relationship. These bases are strategically valuable, projecting power in a region critical for global energy transport and fighting terrorism. France likes to consider itself a supporter of international law and human rights, but its military presence in the Gulf implies a willingness to prioritise geopolitical interests. The naval presence affords France (and, by extension, the EU) leverage over those sea lanes but also gets them involved in regional conflicts and, to some extent, the authoritarianism that exists in parts of the Gulf.

Table (3): EU-GCC Trade, Investment, and Energy Relations Over the Decades

Year	EU Exports to GCC (USD Billion)	EU Imports from GCC (USD Billion)	EU FDI in GCC (USD Billion)
1995	10.2	10.5	23.5
2011	38	62	23.5
2022	22	22	null

EU-GCC Trade, Investment, and Energy Relations Over the Decades

Compromises in EU-Gulf Relations

Navigating the landscape where security and economic advantages brush against stated global commitments often necessitates compromise. Germany and France, for example, reflect a larger trend among European nations: in their engagement with Gulf states, trade, investments, and security interests frequently take precedence [32]. This friction between stated ideals and practical actions has drawn criticism from human rights organisations and diplomats who argue for a more consistent policy. However, the core problem stems from the significant economic and energy dependencies connecting these regions. For decades, policymakers have walked a fine line, seeking to balance export opportunities and strategic positioning with the need to support democratic ideals—a balancing act evident in both corporate discussions and governmental decisions [33].

Understanding the subtle interplay between trade, military alliances, and human rights provides both academics and practitioners with insight into why specific EU policies may appear inconsistent. It also underscores the inherent challenges to creating a foreign policy that fulfils both economic imperatives and moral ambitions. For observers tracking EU-Gulf relations, examining these cases brings to light how power and pragmatism often eclipse principle, thus influencing a partnership shaped by the world's varied and often conflicting priorities. In considering the EU's ties with the Gulf, one should remember the intimate connection between energy security and wider geopolitical strategies. For both academics and journalists, this implies looking beyond official pronouncements to discern the underlying interests guiding decision-making. Entrepreneurs and diplomats similarly can gain from acknowledging the tensions at play, allowing for more insightful strategies that anticipate future compromises and contradictions.

Table (4): *EU-GCC Economic and Trade Relations*

	Value
20% of the global economy	
17.5%	
50%	

EU-GCC Economic and Trade Relations

Shifting Dynamics: From Partnership to Strategic Competition

The dynamics linking the European Union and the Gulf have seen substantial shifts over the years. Early on, the foundation was built on shared values, including diplomacy, human rights, and collaboration across nations. The aim was to create partnerships based on shared interests and principles, yielding benefits for both parties [34]. However, this arrangement has since evolved into something more intricate. Economic needs, security concerns, and geopolitical competition have shaped interactions, sometimes giving rise to more cautious dealings between competing interests rather than friendly collaborations. Partnership and rivalry have become blurred, compelling each side to rethink its strategies towards the other.

Recent examples make clear just how much things have changed. Germany's arms sales to Riyadh are a positive example. They have traditionally emphasised strict arms controls and respect for human rights. However, despite its principles, it still sells weapons to Saudi Arabia, a country involved in conflicts and noted for its serious abuses. These deals reflect Germany's need for Gulf energy and stability in the region, which can clash with its stated principles [35]. Likewise, France has maintained a visible naval presence in the UAE, running bases and holding joint drills. Security concerns, economic interests, and the importance of Gulf markets drive France's moves. These instances show that economic and security needs often outweigh the EU's goals of promoting human rights and democracy. In practice, national interests often take precedence over the narratives of values, changing what were once simple partnerships into complex calculations that are often competitive.

The Shifting Dynamics of Global Influence

This evolution showcases a broader shift in how global actors perceive influence. Countries are more about competitive manoeuvring for their own sake than shared goals (Krahmann, 2018). The Gulf states, crucially, are not mere recipients; they are actively shaping the game (Ulrichsen, 2016). They use energy and location to attract investments, alliances, and support from rival powers (Friedman, 2020). The EU constantly strikes a balance between ideals and realpolitik. It champions human rights and multilateralism, yet is increasingly reliant on Gulf energy, exposing it to influence that sometimes openly questions (Brattberg & Hille, 2021). This tension highlights the evolving international scene, where collaboration and competition mix (Stephen & Dijkink, 2019).

In practical terms, this means that the EU needs to change how it deals with the Gulf. Assuming shared values guarantee easy partnerships is no longer realistic (Rácz, 2020). We need clear strategies that acknowledge the region's dynamic changes in economics, security, and politics (Khodabandeh,

2021). It takes finesse to maintain a human rights focus without pushing away energy partners (Baker, 2022). Perhaps smaller, targeted actions—think promoting transparency in arms agreements or fostering regional talks—could be more effective than expansive, ideal-based methods (Al Ibrahim, 2019). Acknowledging this landscape of competing agendas enables the EU to craft more effective policies that advance its long-term interests without compromising its principles, generally speaking (Meyer, 2021).

4
Normative Power in Practice
EU's Human Rights and Multilateralism Agenda

The European Union, a long-standing advocate of global standards, has consistently demonstrated its dedication to human rights. This commitment is a strong tool in its diplomatic efforts to change how the world is run and encourage cooperation between many countries, especially in the Gulf region.

The EU firmly believes that a strong commitment to human rights and democracy is a key factor in building stability and peace. However, the EU's influence is often constrained by the complex geopolitical dynamics of Gulf countries, where traditional ideas about sovereignty and regional security often take precedence over normative considerations [38]. This circumstance is particularly evident when the EU engages with countries known for their problematic human rights records.

Despite issuing critical reports and setting specific conditions, the EU has found it challenging to implement fundamental changes in countries where strategic interests appear to outweigh normative pledges [39]. Thus, while the EU's dedication to multilateralism and human rights remains a central aspect of its foreign policy, the contrast between its goals and the realities of Gulf politics reveals the limits of its influence, highlighting the difficulties faced by an actor focused on norms in a region marked by conflicting interests and authoritarian forms of government.

EU Policies Promoting Human Rights: Instruments and Limitations

The European Union utilises a variety of strategies to advance human rights worldwide, especially in regions where freedoms face limitations. These strategies include diplomatic dialogues aimed at influencing policies in favour of human rights, legal structures that commit member states to upholding specific norms, and economic tools, such as trade agreements, which can potentially incentivise improved practices [40]. The EU presents itself as a proponent of multilateralism, encouraging nations to cooperate toward common objectives, human dignity and justice [41].

While its rhetoric is a laudable aim, practical implementation often exposes notable discrepancies between intent and actual results. Understanding the nuances of EU policy in the Gulf necessitates taking into account factors beyond the official discourse. The challenge of balancing human rights promotion with managing energy reliance creates inconsistencies that can damage the EU's reputation.

For genuine advancement, the EU must contemplate these difficulties. Thoughtful discussions with member states could help align policy with principles. This analysis does not merely point out deficiencies; it highlights the importance of harmony between values and actions, advocating for a more principled approach in dealings with the Gulf region and beyond.

Table (5): *EU Human Rights Promotion Instruments and Limitations*

Instrument	Description	Limitation	Source
Export Controls on Surveillance Technology	Regulations requiring EU companies to report licensing details for exporting surveillance technology to foreign governments, aiming to prevent human rights abuses.	Inconsistent implementation among member states, with some countries exploiting loopholes, leading to ineffective enforcement.	Booth, A. (2023). Export controls and transparency: The EU's strategy to reduce human rights abuses. Sanford Journal of Public Policy.
Human Rights Defenders (HRDs) Protection Policies	Joint guidance by the U.S. and EU recommending actions for online platforms to protect HRDs from online threats.	Lack of enforcement mechanisms, rendering the recommendations ineffective in safeguarding HRDs.	Empty Promises: Recent Measures to Safeguard Human Rights Defenders Lack Effective Enforcement on Online Platforms. Immigration and Human Rights Law Review.
Human Rights Monitoring Mechanisms	Systems established to monitor and report human rights violations within EU member states.	Limited effectiveness due to insufficient resources and political will, leading to inadequate enforcement of human rights standards.	Training Manual for Human Rights Monitoring - Chapter XVII: Monitoring Economic, Social and Cultural Rights. University of Minnesota Human Rights Library.
EU Charter of Fundamental Rights	A legally binding document outlining the human rights and freedoms protected within the EU.	Challenges in enforcement and application, particularly in member states with differing legal traditions and interpretations.	Maastricht Guidelines on Violations of Economic, Social and Cultural Rights. University of Minnesota Human Rights Library.

EU Human Rights Promotion Instruments and Limitations

Case Studies: Human Rights Advocacy in the Gulf Context

Generally speaking, within Gulf State contexts, advocating for human rights involves navigating a complicated relationship between the European Union's normative influence and the area's deeply rooted Realpolitik. The EU often presents itself as a defender of human rights; however, its impact is limited by the strategic considerations and regional political forces at play.

Collaborations between the EU and the Gulf Cooperation Council's (GCC) countries, for example, tend to emphasise economic and security objectives, occasionally overshadowing democratic ideals, which leads to a somewhat selective approach to human rights initiatives. This is evident in instances where the EU has expressed disapproval of human rights violations yet frequently refrains from imposing stringent sanctions, possibly reflecting a preference for maintaining strategic alliances over comprehensively addressing these abuses.

The EU's dealings with countries like the United Arab Emirates and Saudi Arabia illustrate this point, where energy reliance and military connections tend to take precedence over calls for reform. While the EU attempts to incorporate human rights clauses into trade agreements, the limited willingness of Gulf states to respond to such pressures raises questions about the practical value and believability of these approaches.

Recent studies, for instance, show that incorporating human rights issues into discussions often results in a merely surface-level acceptance of EU standards without corresponding policy adjustments in Gulf nations [42]. Therefore, the conflict between the EU's desire to advance human rights and the real political situations in the Gulf demonstrates the impending need for meaningful improvements in human rights matters [43].

Germany's Relationship with Saudi Arabia

Germany's dealings with Saudi Arabia highlight a significant conflict between the EU's economic interests and its commitment to human rights in the Gulf region. Although German foreign policy ostensibly champions human rights, the actual situation reveals a different narrative. Arms sales provide a stark illustration of where economic practicality often outweighs moral imperatives [44]. Even with international worries concerning Saudi Arabia's military actions in Yemen and numerous accounts of human rights violations, Germany has kept approving arms exports to Riyadh, justifying it by claiming the need to maintain strategic and economic connections [45].

These choices are not isolated; Germany views the Gulf region not only as an important market for its defence sector but also as a partner that aids its energy requirements. These profitable agreements not only sustain domestic employment but also enhance Germany's standing as a prominent global arms supplier. Many advocate stricter regulations on such sales, highlighting the humanitarian consequences of conflicts where German weaponry is allegedly deployed; nonetheless, intense lobbying by defence firms and a reluctance to jeopardise economic partnerships often impede political resolve. Consequently, there is an awkward equilibrium where human rights are discussed, but actions undermine genuine advocacy.

The Broader EU Gulf Policy Problem

Recent studies highlight a broader issue that influences the EU's Gulf policy, particularly in the context of small state foreign policy strategies [46]. Though the EU officially supports things like democracy, human rights, and working together internationally, member states, such as Germany, often find it hard to balance these beliefs with their need for energy and strong economies—a difficulty neoclassical realism describes by emphasising how domestic issues affect foreign policy choices [47].

The situation with Saudi Arabia highlights the drawbacks of these compromises, which prompts people to question whether the EU can be trusted to promote its values when dealing with Gulf nations. It is a stark example that economic considerations frequently play a more decisive role in shaping foreign policy than universal ideals, leading to contradictions that impede potential reforms in the area.

France's Strategic Objectives in the UAE

France's military presence in the UAE, viewed from another angle, underscores the tension between strategic objectives and aspirations for human rights progress. The establishment of French naval bases there undoubtedly indicates a focus on geopolitical influence. Such an objective appears to outweigh prioritising democratic values, particularly as renewed interest in EU-GCC collaboration emphasises overlapping strategic interests [48].

Through this, France can project power in a critical maritime area, thereby strengthening its role in Gulf security and protecting crucial trade routes. Due to its strategic location near the Strait of Hormuz, a key transit point for global oil shipments, the UAE is a pivotal ally for maintaining France's regional influence. However, this closeness has a cost. The UAE's record on civil rights and political freedoms is under scrutiny, given restrictions on dissent and limited space for civil society, which mirrors the broader regional challenge of balancing nation-statehood and historical legacies [49].

Despite these concerns, France has cultivated military ties, seemingly setting aside human rights issues to focus on complex power considerations. This difference between EU ideals and France's actions shows the difficult path of navigating intricate regional dynamics, where security and economic benefits often overshadow commitments to freedom. French officials contend that strong defence cooperation with the UAE advances broader European security, helps counterbalance competing powers, and stabilises the Gulf.

Nevertheless, this exposes contradictions in the EU's policy framework. The bloc strives to promote a model based on the rule of law and human dignity, but a few member states engage in partnerships that contradict these aims. The French case is an example of juggling roles—advocating for values while also being a pragmatic power broker—that risks eroding trust in the EU's broader human rights agenda.

Challenges of Balancing Values and Realpolitik

Navigating the Gulf presents a persistent dilemma, as evident in the cases of Germany and France, where aligning values with the demands of Realpolitik is a challenge. Understanding these inherent tensions is vital for academics, journalists, and policymakers alike when analysing foreign policy complexities in this region [50].

Recent analyses show both countries operate in an environment where ethical ideals frequently conflict with strategic objectives. This highlights the necessity of a finely tuned strategy that accounts for both ethical considerations and geopolitical realities [51].

Indeed, this delicate balance not only impacts diplomatic relations but also shapes perceptions of the EU's role as a catalyst for democratisation and modernisation across the Gulf. In this context, the EU's declared ambitions often conflict with its practical actions, prompting questions among regional players about its commitment and effectiveness.

Evaluating the Effectiveness of the EU's Normative Strategies

The European Union likes to portray itself as a major supporter of human rights, democracy, and international cooperation, often focussing on a vision of influence rooted in shared values and moral leadership. However, in the Gulf region, these ideals often clash with the harsh realities on the ground.

Sometimes, the EU's lofty objectives appear disconnected from its practical actions, exposing a notable discrepancy between its stated beliefs and its actual actions. Brussels often speaks out for good governance and civil liberties. However, it often falls back on quiet diplomacy or economic connections, which prioritise those interests over human rights concerns. This creates a delicate balancing act for many EU member states: how to support core values without compromising access to crucial energy resources or destabilising a geopolitically sensitive region [52].

Some see the situation as a fundamental contradiction, a failure of moral leadership when practical needs take priority over what it believes in. This tension underscores the limitations of the EU's influence in the face of Gulf geopolitics, where strategic alliances and national interests often supersede upholding principles [53].

Upon closer examination, this gap manifests in distinct ways. Diplomatic speeches may extol the virtues of democracy, yet they frequently yield to strategic negotiations centred on oil and security. While high-level statements may denounce repression or human rights abuses, they rarely receive decisive actions or sanctions that could damage economic ties. Imports from the Gulf support the EU's economic health, trapping it between its global image and its energy needs.

This reliance significantly shapes its decision-making more than many want to admit. As a result, Brussels's ability to push for reforms or to take moral positions often turns into simple statements rather than practical steps. These contradictions go beyond mere diplomatic discomfort; they damage the credibility of the EU's message. Advocates wonder whether the EU's influence is truly impactful or merely rhetorical, given that the region's geopolitical realities often overshadow its moral statements.

To fully comprehend the efficacy of the EU's strategies, it is imperative to analyse the practical functioning of influence. Unlike traditional power, which stems from military strength or economic force, the EU relies on soft power—encompassing persuasion, reputation, and the appeal of shared values. However, in the Gulf, this kind of influence often becomes overshadowed by competing interests, as economic dependencies, security concerns, and strategic partnerships often outweigh normative considerations.

For example, the EU's efforts to promote human rights are often overlooked when Gulf states exploit their economic and strategic importance to threaten regional stability or restrict access to vital resources. Countries such as Saudi

Arabia and the UAE utilise their significance as bargaining chips, thereby constraining any European influence grounded in moral authority. This creates a pattern in which the EU's strategies act more as diplomatic talk than as practical tools of influence, often appearing as signs of intent rather than real mechanisms for change.

The focus then shifts from moral persuasion to practical engagement—often at odds with the EU's stated values. The contrast between normative rhetoric and geopolitical reality becomes especially clear when examining specific examples, such as Germany's arms exports to Riyadh, which highlight the challenges of balancing moral principles with practical needs.

5
Gulf Realpolitik
Power, Interests, and Strategic Autonomy

Understanding Gulf States' Foreign Policy Strategies

Germany publicly strives to appear removed from arms deals potentially linked to conflict or human rights abuses. Nevertheless, in practice, a surprising amount of weaponry still ends up in Saudi Arabia. The German government must delicately strike a balance between its professed ethical values and the significant financial gains from arms sales [54]. Critics frequently point out the selective application of Germany's export regulations, where strategic aims often outweigh ethical considerations. Consequently, the EU's declared normative ambitions are sometimes superseded by economic needs and diplomatic pragmatism. The outcome is a situation where moral language is prevalent in speeches but rarely results in actual restrictions, which diminishes the EU's claims of moral leadership. France, on the other hand, presents a different but equally intriguing situation.

French naval bases in the UAE and the broader Gulf region showcase how projecting power can sometimes take precedence over normative ideals [55]. France maintains strategic military bases that reinforce its regional influence and protect its economic interests. These installations symbolise France's dedication to regional security, but they are not primarily about advancing democracy or human rights. Instead, they demonstrate strategic considerations, indicating how France balances its diplomatic goals with military strategy. This presence, some critics observe, complicates the EU's efforts to project a moral image, as military support tends to suggest alignment with existing regimes rather than Brussels' proclaimed values. These bases function more as symbols of firm power than soft influence, suggesting that for some European nations, concrete interests often take precedence over abstract values.

A recurring theme emerges in both examples: the disconnect between the EU's rhetoric and its actions. While European pronouncements prioritise human rights and multilateral cooperation, economic and strategic considerations frequently marginalise these values. These case studies highlight that influence in today's global politics often depends less on moral standing and more on tangible interests. Nations of strategic importance can influence policies and actions, irrespective of their stated ideological commitments. This pattern serves as a constructive reminder that the EU's normative strategies, although appealing in theory, struggle to have a lasting impact in a world where power and interests are, ultimately, the main drivers of decision-making.

For anyone seeking to understand the actual dynamics of influence, these examples underscore that words alone rarely change anything—interests are what truly matter. For those following the EU's influence, the key is to focus on tangible actions, not just rhetoric. Developing actual influence requires a constructive understanding of when the EU's moral language is genuinely supported by action and when it is just for show. Recognising the limitations of soft power in a world where strategic interests come first can help refine expectations. By assessing whether actions match words, countries and analysts can better understand European moves. This approach can help avoid exaggerating the EU's ability to change behaviour based solely on moral appeals, especially in regions where interests tend to come first. Officials and researchers should remember that pursuing influence requires carefully weighing morality and pragmatism, especially in sensitive areas like the Gulf.

Gulf States' Strategic Interests

Gulf states, such as Saudi Arabia, Qatar, and the United Arab Emirates, largely orient their foreign policies around what they perceive as their own strategic advantages. These countries prioritise their regional powers and, above all, their independence. This strategic autonomy often involves navigating a complex international environment, and Western ideals—particularly those focused on human rights and democracy—do not always align perfectly with each other. The tension between Western moral demands and regional aspirations often makes way for pragmatic considerations. When the Arab Spring, for instance, swept through the area, Gulf leaders emphasised stability over the reform that was being called for because they saw democratic movements as a possible threat to their authority. These countries didn't listen to the West's calls for political change. Instead, they used strategies to strengthen their power and silence dissent. Thus, foreign policy decisions often reflect the needs of national stability and security, rather than a strict adherence to democratic values [56]. Case studies, for example, such as Saudi Arabia's arms deals with Western powers, showcase this pragmatic approach.

Germany and France have sold significant arms to the UAE and Riyadh, despite the disturbing human rights record in Yemen. Initially, Germany held back on these sales following the murder of Jamal Khashoggi, but this stance quickly shifted, with geopolitical interests taking precedence. The Saudi deal aimed to bolster defences and sustain regional influence, demonstrating that economic and strategic factors can occasionally eclipse ethical considerations. The UAE's establishment of overseas military bases is another telling example of how Gulf states prioritise power. By securing military bases in nations such as Ethiopia, Somalia, and Egypt, the UAE expands its influence through a robust military presence. This territorial and strategic expansion enables the UAE to project a level of power that complements its economic ambitions and challenges regional rivals, such as Iran. These partnerships are not really about shared values but more about securing a proactive stance in regional conflicts. Analysing the intricate connections between Gulf states and Western nations also reveals a reliance on energy imports, creating a problematic position for the EU concerning human rights. Germany, for example, relies heavily on energy coming from these Gulf nations, which creates a tension between promoting human rights and securing reliable energy sources [57].

Thus, the formulation of foreign policy becomes a precarious balancing act, where the need for energy security often contradicts the desire to promote democratic reforms, which highlights the Realpolitik nature of the Gulf's geopolitical influence. For a comprehensive understanding of Gulf foreign policy, it is essential to recognise the complex interplay of strategic interests. Engaging with these nations necessitates the acknowledgement that these states operate within a framework shaped by realpolitik. This not only shapes their policies but also influences the perceptions and policies of Western nations as they attempt to navigate a complex and contradictory relationship. By observing these patterns, experts in international relations and diplomacy can prepare more thoroughly for the multifaceted—and often contradictory—nature of interactions with Gulf states.

Energy Sovereignty and Strategic Autonomy in the Gulf States

The Gulf states have long recognised that control over their energy is, essentially, about more than just money; it is, in fact, a bedrock for self-determination and strategic independence [58]. This independence allows them to set their path without being constantly tied to the agendas pushed by distant powers or those international bodies that often impose conditions that clash with what the Gulf actually wants. While many Western nations like to discuss human rights and collaborate globally in their foreign dealings, the Gulf's drive for energy independence often appears to overshadow these ideals, by prioritising the acquisition and maintenance of control over resources and political influence. At the heart of all this is that ongoing tug-of-war between Western values and what is actually happening on the ground in the Gulf. A significant portion of the world's oil and gas comes from the Gulf, making it crucial for global energy.

The leaders there use this power with a precise aim: protecting their independence from outside meddling, which often means forming partnerships that largely disregard criticisms about how they govern or the social freedoms they allow. Energy security, for the Gulf, is not so much about lofty ideals but more about, well, power that you can actually see and feel: the power to mess with global markets, have influence in the region, and keep things stable at home. Look at the Gulf's move towards energy sources that are not just oil, such as investments in renewable energy and energy

THE EU'S LIMITED LEVERAGE 53

companies around the world; it really highlights this point. States like the UAE and Saudi Arabia are expanding beyond just selling oil, aiming to protect themselves from being hurt by being overly dependent on a single commodity or market. This shows they want to be free from economic and political pressures that come with being so reliant on energy.

Energy security is not just about having enough supply; it is a shield against other countries interfering and a means to steer one's own course. The way the Gulf and Western countries interact really shows how practical considerations often prevail over values. Take the European Union: they talk a lot about working together and human rights, but they also rely heavily on energy from the Gulf [59]. This dependency makes them more cautious when it comes to advocating for changes or criticising policies in the region. Europe's need for energy shows that its influence has limits and that its foreign policy has some contradictions. The Gulf, meanwhile, leverages this reliance to maintain its independence and push back against demands that threaten its autonomy or its objectives in the region. Consider Germany's sales of weapons to Riyadh; it is a clear example of this balance.

Germany says it cares about human rights and has, at times, been concerned about what Saudi Arabia does. However, Germany continues to sell advanced weapons to Riyadh, balancing its ethical obligations with its economic and strategic interests. This situation highlights the tensions in European policy, where trade and security often take precedence over discussions of rights abuses or regional conflicts. Even though there are public debates in Germany about the morality of these sales, the main goal remains to maintain influence and access in a strategically important region.

France's naval presence in the United Arab Emirates is another case, albeit somewhat different. Instead of mainly focusing on selling arms, France uses its military presence to maintain strategic influence. Its naval bases contribute to regional security, while also enabling France to project power and protect trade routes. The UAE values this presence because it helps balance out other players in the region, enhancing its security while strengthening its ties with a significant European power. This arrangement is a beneficial example of diplomatic pragmatism, where staying independent is about having shared interests, not just following what others say is right. These two cases demonstrate the delicate balance between power, interests, and morality. Germany's arms sales and France's military presence demonstrate how the Gulf states approach their relationships with Europe, not by merely complying with expectations, but by engaging in negotiations.

Energy Security and Autonomy in Gulf Politics

Energy security and strategic partnerships are vital instruments for the Gulf states in safeguarding their independence, even when engaging with partners whose stated ideals may not perfectly align with Gulf governance or policies [60]. Gulf leaders prioritise maintaining control over their own destiny when navigating international relationships. They strive to maintain a dominant position in dealings with external powers, by utilising energy resources and regional influence as key bargaining tools. This practical approach has enabled them to resist outside pressure to rapidly alter internal policies or immediately conform to what may be considered universal standards. By ensuring their energy security is sustained, they preserve the freedom to pursue policies on their terms, demonstrating that, in geopolitics, power often carries more weight than pure principle.

Furthermore, energy security is important to understand, as it goes beyond mere supply chains or infrastructure; it is actually deeply connected to political sovereignty, bargaining power, and, national identity [61]. Acknowledging this critical relationship provides a somewhat clearer perspective on why Gulf states tend to react cautiously to external criticism, and also why they cultivate partnerships that strongly uphold their autonomy more so than ideological alignment. For those engaging with the Gulf—this includes diplomats, entrepreneurs, and analysts—understanding the primacy of energy security certainly offers a really pragmatic lens through which to interpret the region's actions and policies.

Balancing External Influences: US, China, Russia, and the EU

The European Union frequently voices strong support for human rights and multilateral diplomacy. However, these principles often clash with its energy requirements. The EU has for a long time relied substantially on imports from Gulf nations, specifically oil and gas from countries such as Saudi Arabia, Qatar, and the United Arab Emirates [62]. This reliance puts the EU in a tricky position, where its stated ideals conflict with its practical needs. For example, even as official statements condemn human rights violations, Europe continues to purchase hydrocarbons from the Gulf, effectively funding regimes with problematic histories [62]. Such a dissonance suggests that economic realities often outweigh rhetoric, creating a tension that defines Europe's foreign policy decisions.

Within this network of dependencies, Gulf states have become adept at manoeuvring external powers— the US, China, Russia, and the EU—to secure their strategic objectives. They strive to maintain a certain level of independence by somewhat balancing these powers against each other. Germany's arms sales to Riyadh exemplify a pragmatic approach—exchanging advanced weaponry for valuable agreements, despite reservations from human rights groups. The French military presence in the Gulf area exemplifies an alternative strategy: maintaining footholds, such as naval bases and joint military exercises, that project influence without excessive reliance on any single power [62].

These nations are particularly interested in safeguarding their sovereignty and often use the interests of larger actors to advance their regional goals. This leads to a nuanced form of sovereignty—one that enables them to garner support from various sources while avoiding dependence on any single external actor. This balancing act has a significant impact on the broader international context. The US still holds significant influence through military alliances and also economic connections, though China's increasing presence adds new complexity. Beijing invests considerably in energy infrastructure projects in the Gulf, provides large loans, and promotes a policy of non-interference that appeals to Gulf leaders who are cautious of Western interference [63]. Russia, meanwhile, employs military alliances and energy agreements to maintain its relevance, frequently siding with Gulf nations on matters such as Syria and Middle Eastern stability.

Table (6): *Public Support for Relations Among Major Powers*

Country	Friendly Relations Support (%)	Hostile Relations Support (%)
China	96.5	1.06
Russia	89.3	3.11
United States	81.6	2.94

Public Support for Relations Among Major Powers

6
The Paradox of Dependence
EU's Reliance on Gulf Energy Imports

The European Union's dependence on Gulf energy imports presents a paradoxical situation, particularly in relation to the EU's normative power projection in the region. The EU typically presents itself as a promoter of democratic values and human rights. However, its need for Gulf energy creates a tension, frequently resulting in a pragmatic approach. The bloc prioritises economic security, at times, over strict adherence to its own stated ideals. [64]. This dynamic becomes particularly visible in the Persian Gulf's geopolitical arena, where the ongoing negotiation between energy security concerns and political influence continually shapes the EU's strategy when dealing with these oil-rich nations.

Furthermore, this dependence can render the EU vulnerable to Gulf Realpolitik, where the differing goals among EU member states may compromise the EU's ability to present a unified and principled approach to foreign policy [65]. As a result, the EU's energy dependence raises questions about its ability to maintain a consistent normative framework while managing the complex power dynamics that shape its engagement with the Gulf states.

Quantifying Energy Dependency: Data and Trends

Over the years, the European Union has become increasingly reliant on the Gulf states for its energy needs. Upon examining the numbers, a clear picture of this growing dependence emerges, particularly when considering the shifting global economy and the push for greener policies. This situation highlights the importance of effective multilateralism for the EU as it navigates tricky international relationships [66]. Around 30% of the EU's oil came from Gulf producers in 2022, and that percentage has been climbing since 2015. Natural gas imports tell a similar story, with Qatar becoming a major supplier. The back-and-forth of international relations means that the energy supply dynamics between the EU and the Gulf are crucial for stability and security. This increasing dependency is not just about numbers; it shows larger trends in energy consumption and geopolitical realities, particularly as the EU aims to promote its standards in international relations [67].

Many EU nations have had a tough time switching to greener energy sources, which keeps them relying on fossil fuels from the Gulf. Take Germany, for example. It has been tweaking its energy policies to reduce its carbon footprint. Simultaneously, its arms sales to Saudi Arabia demonstrate the intricate balance between adhering to ethical principles and fulfilling practical energy requirements. Thus, the statistics paint a picture of sustainability ambitions clashing with immediate energy demands. Geopolitics and energy needs closely intertwine, shaping foreign policy and international relations. The EU's energy imports from the Gulf have had a dual impact, shaping its stance on human rights and multilateralism. France setting up naval bases in the UAE, for instance, shows increased military cooperation driven by energy concerns. This raises some challenging questions: How do we balance our goals for human rights with the reality of energy insecurity? In essence, the EU has been balancing its efforts to ensure energy security with its promotion of human rights and democratic governance.

Table (7): *EU Energy Import Dependency and Gross Avail-*

able Energy (1990-2023)

Year	Energy Import Dependency Ratio (%)	Gross Available Energy (TJ)
1990	50	62.4
1991	50.5	62.1
1992	51.7	60.5
1993	50.3	60.4
1994	51.3	60.1
1995	52.2	62.1
1996	52.7	64.3
1997	53.6	64
1998	55.4	64.4
1999	55	63.8
2000	56.3	64.4
2001	55.8	66.1
2002	56.3	66.2
2003	56.9	67.8
2004	56.9	68.8
2005	57.8	69.1
2006	58.2	69.8
2007	57.2	69
2008	58.4	68.9
2009	57.2	64.7
2010	55.7	67.3
2011	56.3	65.3
2012	54.9	64.4
2013	53.9	63.7
2014	54.4	61.5
2015	56	62.3
2016	56.1	62.9
2017	57.5	64.2
2018	58.1	63.9
2019	60.5	62.9
2020	57.5	57.7
2021	55.5	61.2
2022	62.5	58.5
2023	58.3	56.1

EU Energy Import Dependency and Gross Available Energy (1990-2023)

Implications for the EU's Foreign Policy Autonomy

The European Union often portrays itself as a major supporter of human rights, democracy, and international cooperation. Nevertheless, its dependence on energy resources from the Gulf region creates some notable issues. The Gulf countries, with their abundant oil and gas reserves, wield considerable influence over Europe's energy supply, which can undermine the EU's human rights stance.

To keep a consistent energy supply, the EU often proceeds

cautiously when discussing political or human rights issues in these nations. This delicate balance can expose vulnerabilities in the EU's foreign policy independence, as economic interests occasionally eclipse its dedication to universal values. When the EU tries to pressure Gulf countries on important matters like workers' rights, political oppression, or regional disputes, it encounters a subtle but effective obstacle: the conflict between its moral standards and the practical demands of economic reliance [68], [69].

EU Foreign Policy and Energy Dependency

The EU's normative influence in the Gulf region is limited because it relies heavily on the region for its energy needs. This dependency makes it reluctant to impose strict sanctions or take firm positions, fearing possible energy supply disruptions or increased costs [70]. A subtle conflict arises between advocating for value-driven foreign policies and protecting energy security. Gulf nations adeptly exploit this power during diplomatic talks, resulting in situations where practical considerations often supersede ethical standards. The EU's foreign policy, inevitably, adapts to changing energy landscapes, which raises doubts about its actual independence given these economic constraints [71]. For instance, Germany's engagement with Saudi Arabia demonstrates how business interests can muddy foreign policy; it persists in arms sales, despite condemnation, reflecting domestic political calculations within strategic alliances. This highlights the challenge of aligning policy with moral principles.

Similarly, France maintains a military presence in the UAE,

navigating the tricky balance between security collaboration and concerns about political oppression. Consequently, the EU struggles to project an independent foreign policy, particularly as individual member states pursue their own national goals. This challenge makes pushing for reforms difficult, as it carries the risk of financial repercussions. A broader issue concerns how the EU might restructure its foreign policy to lessen these vulnerabilities. Possible solutions include seeking alternative energy sources, fostering political unity among member states, and implementing more transparent rules regarding arms exports. Acknowledging the connection between energy dependence and diplomatic strategy is a crucial preliminary step toward a foreign policy that upholds EU principles without compromising security or economic well-being. Therefore, policy observers need to closely monitor evolving alliances and economic linkages in the Gulf to grasp Europe's global standing with a sense of urgency.

Strategies for Diversification and Energy Transition

Given the EU's limited influence in the Gulf, diversification and energy transition strategies should align the urgent need for sustainable development with the Realpolitik of Gulf governance. For instance, Saudi Arabia and the UAE must balance their hydrocarbon wealth with the need for investments in renewable energy.

Evidenced by infrastructural projects, including Israeli-Saudi cooperative ventures [72], these nations are deploying modern energy infrastructure for economic diversification and geopolitical influence. A recent study of renewable energy policies in hydrocarbon-rich Arab states also highlights the varying approaches to energy transition, showing the importance of governance models and policy frameworks [73]. As Gulf nations explore partnerships in renewable energy, the EU may identify opportunities for influence if it can align with the practical goals of Gulf states, even amid their complex political realities.

The European Union's Energy Challenges

The European Union's efforts to reduce its reliance on Gulf states for energy have presented a combination of advances and challenges. Renewable energy development, particularly in wind and solar power, has made significant progress. However, substantial energy imports, liquefied natural gas (LNG) from Gulf nations, continue to play a significant role. Political complexities, including human rights concerns and regional conflicts, further complicate these relationships. Discussions with Gulf nations reveal the struggle between economic interests and moral principles. For example, Germany's arms exports to Riyadh demonstrate how economic needs continue to bind Europe to Gulf regimes, even as some member countries question their stance on human rights [75]. Conversely, France adopts a different strategy by maintaining military facilities in the UAE and other Gulf countries, highlighting the region's geopolitical importance.

Energy diversification requires discovering new sources and handling intricate diplomatic scenarios influenced by economic, security, and political considerations. The EU is pursuing a cleaner, more independent energy future, which is driving practical strategies. The growth of renewable energy has become more vigorous, as countries set challenging goals to increase wind, solar, and hydroelectric energy. Transforming the energy system takes time; it requires significant investments in major infrastructure, technology, and grid management. Simultaneously, the EU is investing more in diversification approaches, obtaining supplies from nations outside the Gulf, such as Norway and Azerbaijan, while researching the development of LNG terminals across its member states. Some countries consider nuclear energy a low-carbon option, despite debates regarding safety and waste management.

Additionally, discussions about hydrogen, particularly green hydrogen produced with renewable energy, have gained popularity. These plans create practical methods to decrease reliance while addressing economic realities. Nevertheless, the tension persists, as some policies emphasise energy security over ethical questions tied to Gulf dependencies. Despite these methods, balancing the desire for energy independence with current geopolitical and economic commitments remains a challenge. The EU often grapples with contradictions; it promotes human rights, democracy, and multilateralism, yet remains heavily reliant on Gulf imports, particularly fossil fuels from autocratic governments. These conflicting priorities can cause policy and action contradictions. Germany's arms sales to Saudi Arabia raise questions about whether economic and strategic interests outweigh the EU's values [74].

Similarly, France's military presence in the Gulf underscores regional security concerns that have a significant impact on European policies. Moving forward, according

THE EU'S LIMITED LEVERAGE 67

to experts, stronger relationships with various energy suppliers, growing domestic renewable capacity, and promoting global cooperation on clean energy projects could help reconcile differences. Transparent dialogue and consistent policy signals can bridge the gap between idealism and Realpolitik. Energy sector stakeholders who strategically focus on renewable and local sources may create a buffer against geopolitical instability and enable a more sustainable, less conflicted energy future.

7
Case Study
Germany's Arms Sales to Riyadh

Considering German arms sales to Riyadh and the EU's limited influence, it is essential to understand the complex relationship between what is considered right and the practical realities of the Gulf region. Germany is committed to human rights and has generally avoided selling weapons to countries in conflict. However, the strategic importance of Saudi Arabia, a key player in the Gulf region, cannot be overstated. The issue creates a challenging situation for German leaders, where strategic interests often outweigh moral concerns. This example illustrates how money can sometimes take precedence over values. Selling weapons generates revenue and helps Germany maintain its competitiveness in the global arms market. Saudi Arabia makes this decision, arguing that its military actions in Yemen are necessary to combat terrorism and uphold stability. The move makes it harder for Europe to impose sanctions or regulations on arms sales [76].

Additionally, the rise of U.S. shale oil and shifts in energy markets have influenced Germany's approach. The EU might want to promote specific values, but practical concerns often lead to continued arms sales. Such selling is done to keep important relationships and benefit the economy. The economic benefits of arms sales cannot be overstated, as they significantly contribute to Germany's economy and help maintain important diplomatic relationships. Ultimately, such activity underscores the limitations of the EU's influence in the region [77].

Historical Overview of German Arms Exports to Saudi Arabia

The narrative of German arms sales to Saudi Arabia is a complicated mix of security needs, economic factors, and diplomatic strategies, reflecting the broader dynamics of power politics in the Gulf. After World War II, Germany gradually resumed its role as a significant arms seller by building alliances, with Gulf monarchies seeking to strengthen their armies amid regional conflicts. The relationship gained momentum in the early 2000s, especially after 9/11, as Saudi Arabia intensified its anti-terrorism efforts and regional stability. German exports peaked in 2011, following the Arab Spring, when Saudi Arabia sought advanced military technology to protect its borders and enhance its regional influence [78].

However, this growing arms trade coincided with increased scrutiny of human rights violations and the impact of military actions, particularly as Saudi Arabia became deeply involved in the protracted conflict in Yemen. This situation highlights the limits of the EU's influence based on values and the challenges it faces in balancing ethical foreign policy with the practical needs of Gulf states, where power politics often outweighs moral concerns [79]. A historical overview of German arms exports to Saudi Arabia reveals the complexity of balancing moral obligations with strategic interests, as well as the inherent conflicts within European security and foreign policy systems.

Table (8): *Historical Overview of German Arms Exports to Saudi Arabia*

Year	Export Volume (Million Euros)
2017	450
2018	0
2022	16.7
2023	36

Historical Overview of German Arms Exports to Saudi Arabia

The Relationship between Germany and Saudi Arabia on Arms Exports

The history of arms exports connecting Germany and Saudi Arabia has fairly old origins, tracing back to the late 20th century. German sales were initially somewhat limited, a reflection of a cautious stance influenced by its post-World War II mindset and a general commitment to pacifism. However, in the 1970s, the discovery of substantial oil reserves in Saudi Arabia significantly altered the situation. German engineering and know-how, then combined with Saudi financial power, resulted in defence agreements that generally grew over subsequent decades.

These deals often featured exports such as tanks, fighter jets and submarines, all of which helped solidify a strategic alliance. Geopolitical events, particularly by the early 2000s, further strengthened this bond. The U.S.-led military involvement in the Middle East has generated fresh security concerns for Saudi Arabia, leading to an increased demand for more advanced military resources. Germany, spotting a possible opportunity, began to more closely align its economic goals with Saudi Arabia's security requirements. The supply of military equipment became a means of encouraging broader bilateral relationships, thereby allowing both countries to benefit politically and economically. It is essential to recall that the rise in the arm's trade was not merely a business transaction; it was also a crucial component of a broader diplomatic strategy to stabilise the region, grounded in mutual interests. German arms exports to Saudi Arabia, in most cases, pose a puzzle within German foreign policy. On the one hand, Germany has often publicly supported human rights and democratic ideals and has a reputation as a leader in promoting these principles in international settings.

On the other hand, when it engages in arms exports to a nation with a notable record of human rights abuses, it raises some uncomfortable ethical questions. It challenges the positive narrative it often attempts to present. This tension is particularly highlighted within the European Union's own multifaceted approach, which seeks to balance energy imports from Gulf nations with a commitment to those human rights principles. EU member states, Germany included, are reliant on Gulf oil, which can put them in a somewhat unstable situation where financial benefits can, at times, overshadow moral concerns.

Adding another layer to this relationship, there is the Franco-German approach to arms policy. Even as Germany has increased its exports to Saudi Arabia, France has strengthened its position through military facilities in the UAE, illustrating a different strategy – combining defence with a stronger diplomatic presence. Both countries navigate the difficulties of arms sales with a deep awareness of their impact on EU-Gulf relations. The problem is clear: for Europe, balancing the need for energy and arms trade with the high-minded aims of human rights remains a delicate and challenging task to achieve. In the final analysis, Germany's experience exporting arms to Saudi Arabia can illustrate how nations may have to walk a tightrope between their ideals and practical realities. As the world continues to grapple with the effects of such decisions, policymakers must consider how best to balance ethical considerations with important strategic interests. Understanding these relationships, including their contradictions, will be crucial for effective diplomatic negotiations going forward.

Legal and Ethical Dilemmas: Human Rights versus Business Interests

The export of German arms to Riyadh highlights a tension between what is legally required and what is ethically sound. German law generally places strict restrictions on who can purchase weapons, particularly if they are involved in conflicts or have a less-than-stellar human rights record [82]. However, things do not always work out as planned.

Even with the worries about the Yemen War and claims that Saudi military actions have led to civilian deaths—there have been quite a few allegations [83]—German firms have, in most cases, kept selling arms to Saudi Arabia. This ongoing arms trade raises some tricky ethical questions. Does the legal framework effectively halt arms exports to regions where human rights violations occur? It appears that a divide exists between what the law intends and what actually happens in practice within the arms industry.

Balancing Human Rights and Commercial Interests

Balancing human rights with export interests presents a particularly sharp challenge, especially given that economic motivations and established diplomatic relationships frequently underpin these sales [84]. These decisions put a strain on the legal system and raise fundamental questions about the moral bearings of governments and societies. Germany's situation reveals how Realpolitik—the lure of jobs, industrial expansion, and strategic alliances—can sometimes overshadow legal commitments, shifting priorities away from human rights [85]. Europe's broader ethical challenge embodies a delicate balancing act. On one hand, the European Union strives to promote human rights and champion multilateral cooperation.

On the other hand, its member states are significantly reliant on Gulf nations, both as vital trading partners and for energy security. These Gulf regimes, often criticised for their restrictions on political freedoms and general repression, exert considerable influence due to their vast oil and gas reserves. This dependency creates a problematic situation for the EU: should they prioritise robust trade and energy deals, or strongly advocate for political reforms and respect for human dignity?

France's naval deployment in the UAE offers a similar picture. Maintaining strategic military cooperation and access to naval bases secures France's regional influence, but it also necessitates collaboration with governments whose human rights records may raise concerns. This partnership presents challenges for advocating democracy or critiquing internal repression. The contradiction becomes obvious when economic and security considerations quieten critical voices or weaken diplomatic pressure. Europe's aspiration for a consistent foreign policy often conflicts with the need to ensure energy supplies and maintain commercial ties, leaving principles in a sort of limbo between aspiration and reality. These ethical and legal dilemmas have tangible repercussions for individuals living under oppressive regimes and for the overall credibility of the European project.

When weapons sold by Germany end up fuelling conflicts and causing widespread suffering, or when European nations prioritise military bases over calls for human rights, the signal sent to both local communities and the international community is hard to miss. It suggests a prioritisation of commerce and strategic interests over fundamental freedoms [84]. For those observing these dynamics—academics, diplomats, and entrepreneurs—the lesson is evident: navigating Gulf-EU relations demands acknowledging the realities on the ground and making difficult choices [85]. Enhancing transparency in arms deals, carefully evaluating political alliances, and providing genuine support for civil society can help balance these often-competing objectives. Ultimately, reconciling human rights with commercial interests tests Europe's identity and the values it aims to uphold on the global stage.

One practical step involves increasing public scrutiny of arms deals and trade agreements. When citizens, journalists, and policymakers demand greater transparency and accountability, it becomes more difficult for governments to disregard ethical considerations. Monitoring mechanisms and civil society involvement can act as a counterweight to purely economic calculations in shaping foreign policy.

Investing in alternative energy sources can also reduce reliance on Gulf hydrocarbons, allowing for a more principled stance on human rights. For anyone involved—from academics to entrepreneurs—understanding that commercial interests should not trump human dignity is the initial step toward genuine and lasting change.

Impact on Germany's Diplomatic Credibility and EU relationships

Germany's ongoing arms exports to Saudi Arabia have sparked considerable disagreement, not only within German diplomacy but also throughout the broader European Union. Berlin often portrays itself as a proponent of human rights and ethical standards; however, its arms transactions with Riyadh somewhat compromise that perception. Critics point out that these deals seem to send mixed messages [86]. It also brings up questions about how effective European foreign policy really is, since ethical standards seem to be getting pushed aside in favour of geopolitical and economic benefits [87]. These kinds of contradictions do not just affect Germany's reputation in the EU; they also highlight the complexity of arms trade policies, especially now that everyone is paying close attention to human rights.

Germany's Contradictory Foreign Policy

Germany, on the one hand, condemns violence and champions ethical benchmarks, yet also appears to benefit from the very weaponry that potentially fuels conflicts that contradict these standards (MacDonald, 2021). This discrepancy begins to erode Germany's standing as Europe's moral compass, thereby prompting concerns about the cohesiveness of its foreign policy (Hoffmann, 2022). It is true that when trusted allies notice seeming contradictions in national actions, trust at the diplomatic level can indeed suffer (Smith, 2023). If Germany's actions don't align with its rhetoric, it becomes increasingly challenging to lead on human rights (Jones, 2021).

Germany's position on arms sales within the EU may underscore a more pervasive challenge: reconciling financial interests with ethical standards (Thompson, 2020). The EU often pushes for unified approaches to human rights and ethical behaviour; however, member countries will sometimes chart their own courses independently (Klein, 2022). As a significant economy, Germany significantly influences EU policy; nonetheless, arms sales to regimes with questionable human rights records can spark disagreement (Reiter, 2023). Some nations fear Germany's moves might undermine collective EU human rights efforts globally, while others worry about potentially setting a detrimental precedent that inspires similar actions in other nations (Davis, 2021).

As diplomatic partners, consistency is key; when Germany's actions and EU principles appear to be at odds, trust can erode, complicating the development of a unified foreign policy (Turner, 2023). Crucially, this trust relies on a shared perception of moral standards among EU members (Gomez, 2021). Many view the EU as embodying shared principles; however, internal disagreements over arms deals, energy reliance, and differing diplomatic agendas reveal contradictions (Schmidt, 2022). For instance, France's naval presence in the UAE takes a different approach, focussing more on energy security and influence than on strictly moral issues (Brouwer, 2022). This instance shows how countries can prioritise varying foreign policy aspects. When one state's actions clash with collectively agreed values, it could create division, thereby weakening the EU's overall diplomatic position (Peterson, 2020). Without a cohesive approach to issues like arms exports or partnerships, maintaining a reputation of reliability and principle is undeniably challenging (White, 2019).

For Germany, ensuring credibility involves more than just handling the current fallout; it needs deliberate effort to align its financial aims with moral pledges while also openly communicating such policies to EU allies and the global stage (Barker, 2023). This could involve more transparent arms export criteria or proactively engaging in discussions about balancing economic and ethical goals (Fields, 2021). More broadly, for the EU as a whole, fostering a shared understanding aids in rebuilding trust; coordinated policies that balance national concerns with common values might bolster the EU's global standing, thus strengthening its diplomatic power (Martinez, 2022). Ultimately, credibility hinges on consistency and transparency, particularly when managing relationships with resource-rich strategic partners in volatile regions (Fischer, 2023).

8
Case Study
French Naval Bases in the UAE

Strategic Rationale for French Military Presence in the Gulf

France's military presence in the UAE is a linchpin of its strategy to remain relevant in the Gulf, particularly given the ever-changing geopolitics and security situation [90]. The UAE—important both geopolitically and economically—is a key ally in addressing some emerging threats.

The UAE, with its geopolitical significance and economic vitality, provides France an essential base to project power and protect its interests in a time of rising security challenges. In an area marked by shifting alliances and emerging threats, France seeks to solidify its connections through military cooperation [91]. The French government views the presence of troops and military equipment in the UAE not only as a deterrent against regional adversaries, but also to strengthen its ties with the UAE. This connection is based on common goals, such as fighting terrorism and keeping the seas safe.

The region's complexities are profound. With conflicts in Syria and Yemen, coupled with tensions involving Iran, the strategic landscape is fraught with risks. France aims to be a stabilising force through either its actions or strategies. Military exercises, initiatives, and cooperation agreements signal its commitment to Gulf stability while countering radicalism. Involving other nations in joint drills amplifies France's role as a key player in promoting security in the area. This approach fosters relationships with both local authorities and European allies, enabling France to enhance its collaborative efforts in various scenarios.

The establishment of French naval bases within the UAE is a testament to France's strategic foresight in enhancing its operational capabilities in the Gulf. These bases, strategically located, ensure rapid response to threats, reinforcing France's position as a major player in Gulf security dynamics. The French Navy's presence signifies a commitment to maritime security, which is vital for safeguarding key shipping routes in a region where sea-based commerce plays a crucial role in the global economy. France's naval strength complements the efforts of Gulf states in protecting their interests against piracy and potential military confrontations.

In this context, it serves as a reminder of how military infrastructure functions tactically and carries strategic weight in international relations. French naval bases play a critical dual role as a tool for projecting power and as a component for cooperative security, shaping the security discussions and decisions made in the Gulf. Such positioning enhances France's credibility and helps in addressing the complex relationship between interests within the region, making its military presence a cornerstone of its foreign policy.

Implications for Regional Security and the EU's Influence

France is actively working to deepen its relationships in a region known for its ever-changing allegiances and the emergence of new threats. Its troop presence and military hardware in the UAE are not just about deterring potential adversaries. Instead, it is also a way to build stronger connections based on mutual concerns, which include counterterrorism efforts as well as maritime security matters [92].

The area is incredibly complex, with ongoing conflicts in places like Syria and Yemen, plus tensions involving Iran, all contributing to a challenging strategic environment. France aims to act as a stabilising force. France achieves this through military exercises and cooperation agreements, demonstrating its commitment to maintaining stability in the Gulf region and combating radicalism. When France involves other countries in joint drills, it enhances its position as a crucial player in promoting regional security. Such collaborative efforts help nurture relationships with both local powers and European allies, allowing France to bolster collaborative initiatives across various scenarios. The establishment of French naval bases in the UAE shows strategic foresight. It enhances operational capabilities in the Gulf, facilitating swift responses to threats and strengthening France's role in the region's security dynamics.

The French Navy's presence underscores its commitment to maritime security, which is essential for protecting vital shipping lanes in an area where sea-based commerce is crucial to the global economy. The French navy's presence helps Gulf states protect their interests from piracy and possible military conflicts. Thus, military infrastructure serves both tactical purposes and holds strategic significance in international relations. The French naval bases serve as both a means of projecting power and a component of cooperative security. This dual role is vital in shaping security discussions and decisions within the Gulf, enhancing France's credibility. The French government also addresses the complex interplay of interests within the region, making its military presence a key part of its foreign policy. The French naval bases in the UAE represent more than just a military presence in the Gulf. It reflects an apparent effort to anchor France—and thus the EU—in a strategically important area. These bases allow the French navy to maintain a steady presence near critical maritime points such as the Strait of Hormuz.

A significant portion of the global oil trade passes through this point, enabling France to project its power and safeguard maritime routes. This also makes it possible to quickly respond to crises like piracy and wars between states. They also serve as a platform for combined operations with Gulf partners, strengthening ties with key players such as the UAE, which seeks security assurances amid regional tensions and shifting alliances. The bases serve as both a symbol and a tool of France's commitment to regional stability; amid simmering tensions between Iran, Saudi Arabia, and other Gulf states, such footholds provide leverage for deterring hostility and ensuring that European interests remain protected in an often volatile neighbourhood. The sea lanes monitored from these installations are not merely commercial arteries but strategic lifelines for energy supplies critical to European economies. Beyond military readiness, the bases enhance intelligence sharing and coordination on issues such as counterterrorism, thereby offering a degree of collective security. This presence signals to other external powers—namely the United States, China, and Russia—that Europe seeks a more active role in the Gulf's future, even as its influence faces intense competition [93].

European Engagement in the Gulf: Strategic Tensions

The EU's engagement with the Gulf reveals a core tension: a region resistant to outside influence, yet internally fragmented. Consider France's naval presence in the UAE. The EU champions human rights, democracy, and multilateralism, but its strategic and economic needs often dictate a more pragmatic approach. Gulf states, the UAE and Saudi Arabia, face criticism for their human rights records and restrictive governance; however, Europe relies heavily on their energy exports and trade agreements. This results in a contradiction: European nations publicly endorse normative ideals while privately collaborating with Gulf autocracies. France's military bases in the Gulf demonstrate a prioritisation of strategic interests over stated EU principles—a broader trend in European foreign policy [94]. Similarly, Germany continues arms sales to Saudi Arabia, despite condemnation over actions in Yemen and civilian casualties [95].

These examples show how hard it is for the EU to balance its values-based self-image with the Gulf's political and economic realities. While the naval bases afford France—and, therefore, the EU—some leverage, this typically translates into subtle influence rather than overt pressure for reform or human rights. European governments must delicately balance their needs for Gulf cooperation in energy, security, and migration, while these dependencies limit their capacity to drive change. As a result, strategic patience and selective engagement often outweigh bold interventions that align with the EU's rhetoric.

The dynamics surrounding France's naval bases and Germany's arms sales raise vital questions about Europe's global role. Can the EU genuinely influence the Gulf's future in line with its values, or will it risk becoming a passive participant, sacrificing its ideals for pragmatism? The answer is likely somewhere in between. Though the naval bases provide a deeper engagement foothold, they may also entangle Europe further in a conflict-ridden, authoritarian region. For analysts and policymakers alike, this complexity necessitates a continuous reassessment of how Europe can exert influence without compromising its publicly championed principles.

Observers should carefully monitor how the EU balances energy diversification with security commitments in the Gulf. The transition to renewable energy and reduced fossil fuel imports could gradually lessen Europe's vulnerability, potentially enabling a firmer stance on human rights. Until such shifts occur, the EU's influence will often manifest through incremental gains and quiet diplomacy, rather than sweeping reforms. Awareness of these tensions is crucial for understanding Europe's actions in the Gulf and predicting future developments in regional security and diplomacy.

Balancing Alliances: France, the UAE, and Broader EU Interests

The strategic partnership between France and the UAE effectively balances military goals and economic considerations in the Gulf region. French naval bases, especially the one in Abu Dhabi, play a key role in this. Horne (2015) notes that these bases enable France to exert influence in the region, protect vital shipping lanes, and support counter-terrorism efforts. Simultaneously, shared economic goals such as defence supplies, infrastructure development, and investments propel France's involvement with the UAE [Meyer, 2020]. This partnership illustrates a delicate balancing act in the region, where military presence is closely tied to economic cooperation, reflecting the intricate nature of international relations in the Gulf (Thomas, 2021), as Bardot (2019) explains.

To secure influence without overcommitting, this relationship demonstrates a regional balancing act, combining military presence with economic diplomacy. This relationship exemplifies the delicate interplay between traditional military alliances and economic ties, where each reinforces the other.

Within this context, the broader European Union faces a tough challenge: how to stay influential in Gulf affairs while upholding a moral stance rooted in human rights and multilateral values. Many European countries, like Germany, prioritise diplomatic approaches that emphasise human rights and multilateral agreements. Nevertheless, this stance often clashes with their energy dependence on Gulf oil and gas, which keeps these countries connected to the Gulf's geopolitics. For instance, Germany's recent arms sales to Saudi Arabia reveal a tension. While Germany lectures on abiding by international law and protecting human rights, it still ships weapons to a region marked by conflict and restrictions on freedoms. This contradiction highlights the challenge of upholding principled diplomacy when economic and energy interests clash with those very ideals.

French naval bases in the UAE serve as a practical tool for France to stay relevant in Gulf security arrangements, a move that often stands at odds with the EU's broader push for moral leadership. France seeks to preserve its influence in the region, partly to shield its economic ventures and reinforce its strategic autonomy.

EU countries find themselves caught between promoting human rights and multilateralism while simultaneously relying on Gulf energy. This creates a delicate balancing act, akin to walking a tightrope, where each step impacts regional stability and European diplomatic credibility. Such a scenario highlights the challenge of balancing security interests with the EU's moral authority. One approach is fostering regional dialogues that include Gulf countries on human rights and climate issues, alongside security cooperation, to build bridges without sacrificing core principles. This combination of pragmatism and values can help Europe identify a sustainable path amid competing priorities.

9
Challenges to EU's Normative Authority in the Gulf

Economic diplomacy seeks influence carefully, without excessive commitment. Think of traditional military alliances and economic ties – they interact fascinatingly, each reinforcing the other, almost like a delicate dance [98]. Now, consider the broader European Union. It faces a significant challenge: how to remain influential in Gulf affairs while upholding its commitment to human rights and multilateral values—many EU nations, including Germany, favour diplomatic strategies that emphasise human rights and international agreements. But, and it is a significant but, this principled position often clashes with their need for Gulf oil and gas. This keeps them tangled up in Gulf geopolitics.

Take Germany's recent arms sales to Saudi Arabia, for example. Here is the tension: Germany champions international law and human rights, yet it sells weapons to a region known for conflict and limited freedoms. This contradiction highlights the difficulty of maintaining principled diplomacy when economic and energy needs conflict with those very principles [99]. Similarly, France keeps naval bases in the UAE. This is a pragmatic approach for France to remain involved in Gulf security, which sometimes conflicts with the EU's broader goal of moral leadership. France seeks to maintain its influence in the region, partly to safeguard its economy and enhance its strategic autonomy.

Meanwhile, EU countries find themselves in a tricky spot – they want to promote human rights and multilateralism, but they also rely on Gulf energy. It is like walking a tightrope, where every step affects regional stability and the credibility of Europe. So, here is a key question: how can they support security interests without hurting the EU's moral authority? One approach might be to encourage regional talks that involve Gulf countries in discussions on human rights, climate change, and security cooperation. This could help build relationships without sacrificing core values. This mix of practicality and values could help Europe find a sustainable path forward, even with competing priorities.

Selective Engagement: Human Rights vs. Energy and Security Interests

The European Union, while a self-proclaimed advocate for human rights and multilateral cooperation, sometimes sees its energy policies and security aims at odds with these core values (Smith, 2021). Geopolitical realities can lead the EU to prioritise securing energy and forging alliances, potentially at the expense of its ethical commitments, as noted by Jones & García (2022). A perplexing narrative emerges: grand human rights ideals sometimes seem secondary to practical needs (Miller, 2020). Specifically, economic connections to Gulf states, particularly in the energy sector, compel EU members to carefully balance their ethical positions with the pragmatic realities of international interactions (O'Brien, 2023).

For example, as Europe pivots toward greener energy and diversifies its sources, it cannot simply dismiss the considerable leverage wielded by Gulf nations rich in oil (Thompson, 2021). The bond between Europe and the Gulf is clear; oil and gas from the region are essential for both industrial activity and the continent's economic health (Ahmed, 2023). As EU nations participate in trade and partnership negotiations, their commitment to ethical foreign policy may occasionally become less prominent. This reveals a somewhat selective approach, in which human rights considerations are not always prioritised (Brown, 2022). Germany's arms exports to Saudi Arabia serve as a notable illustration of this delicate balance, revealing the complications that arise when ethical standards intersect with geopolitical imperatives (Davis, 2023).

Ethical Implications of Arms Exports and Military Presence

Germany asserts its dedication to upholding human rights. Yet, arms sales persist to nations under fire for their human rights conduct, notably concerning the conflict in Yemen. This inconsistency casts doubt on the genuine nature of Germany's ethical commitments because profitable agreements often seem to outweigh moral considerations related to human rights. Arms exports, in this view, become essential for sustaining diplomatic relationships and ensuring financial gains, despite the worrying effects on human rights [102].

France's naval bases in the UAE, in a similar vein, highlight a complex interplay involving security considerations and moral principles. Establishing a military presence in the Gulf, France seeks reinforced alliances aimed at regional stability. While justifiable as a means of combating terrorism and enhancing security, such actions entail significant ethical trade-offs. France must manage its relationship with a nation under scrutiny for human rights issues globally. The deployment of French forces demonstrates conflicting motivations, including the pursuit of security and energy independence, which may undermine the EU's commitment to human rights.

These examples are not one-off occurrences, signalling a broader trend in EU foreign policy. The tension between ethical desires and practical energy/security needs creates a context where the EU's standing as a champion of human rights is increasingly uncertain [103]. For policymakers and researchers, the challenge involves reconciling these different goals and finding methods to support human rights without jeopardising vital energy ties. A principled and consistent strategy requires diplomatic action to be considered alongside its broader effects on global human rights standards.

Perception of Double Standards and Credibility Issues

The European Union has, for many years, styled itself as a champion of democracy, multilateralism, and, importantly, human rights [1]. However, its deep economic links with Gulf energy producers introduce a conflict that, in some respects, undermines this moral authority [2]. Securing vital oil and gas supplies from the Gulf forces a tricky balancing act – advocating human rights alongside the need for energy security [3]. This contradiction, observers have increasingly noted, appears to be a double standard [4]. Indeed, when the EU condemns specific actions in the Middle East but then sustains close economic relationships with what some might describe as autocratic governments, its pronouncements can start to seem disingenuous [5].

This tension between ideals and what some consider

hard-nosed interests is a source of consternation for external critics, as well as for many within the EU who anticipate a consistent foreign policy [6]. Given the wealth and geopolitical influence of the Gulf, European politicians often appear to value supply security and regional stability over strictly principled positions [7]. As a result, the EU's pronouncements regarding the rule of law and human rights may sound less convincing [8].

Populations whom the EU claims to support can interpret these declarations as empty words, quickly forgotten when energy or security concerns emerge [9]. This divergence between stated values and Realpolitik choices fuels scepticism about the EU's actual commitments, reducing its prior influence in global diplomacy [10]. Critically, this perception of a hypocritical stance affects more than its public image; it creates real issues for the EU in its dealings with the Gulf region, where trust is paramount [11]. The European role in human rights dialogues risks becoming ineffective—dismissed due to apparent contradictions or strategic neglect [12]. The EU's challenge mirrors a more widespread problem faced by democracies trying to balance advocating for reform with the demands of practical necessities [13].

Credibility Challenges in EU-Gulf Relations

The EU's credibility, in its complex engagement with Gulf partners, is constantly being shaped by its decisions and oversights, as noted by Crisp [1]. Consider, for instance, the persistent controversy surrounding Germany's arms sales to Saudi Arabia. Despite publicly voicing concerns about the humanitarian crisis in Yemen and advocating for arms export restrictions, Germany has continued to approve substantial weapons deals with Riyadh (Schmitz, 2020). This practice suggests a potential prioritisation of economic interests and influence over concerns about serious abuses, thus undermining Germany's role as a champion of human rights within the EU context (Clausen, 2022). This discrepancy often draws criticism from both civil society and other EU member states, raising questions about the extent to which economic considerations should outweigh ethical principles (Bader & Möller, 2021).

France, another significant European power, adopts a different approach, maintaining a military presence in the Gulf, notably through naval bases in the United Arab Emirates (UAE) (Heisbourg, 2020). France's dedication to security partnerships and its regional influence has led to stronger military ties in the Gulf, promoting defence cooperation and shared operations (Duchâtel, 2021). While this engagement provides strategic benefits for France, it also presents similar credibility challenges. Given the UAE's track record on freedoms and labour rights, France's visible military presence could be interpreted as tacit support, complicating its efforts to promote democratic values internationally (Kälin, 2019; Talapessy, 2022).

These instances – German arms exports to Riyadh and French naval bases in the UAE – illustrate the broader credibility struggles the EU faces. As Fischer notes, economic and strategic interests can sometimes clash with, and even overshadow, stated foreign policy objectives. When one EU country sells arms to a regime accused of war crimes, and another forges military links with an authoritarian state, the message becomes somewhat muddled (Peters, 2021). The

EU's capacity to present a united and principled front can appear fractured, leading to internal divisions and external scepticism (López & Gier, 2021).

Such fragmentation weakens the EU's ability to negotiate reforms or push for improvements in human rights within the Gulf region. Managing these contradictions presents real challenges, as Jörgensen suggests. Navigating between securing energy supplies and wielding influence that reflects the EU's core values requires some care (Jörgensen, 2021). Greater transparency regarding these tensions could foster a more candid conversation, enabling stakeholders to assess the trade-offs with greater realism and objectivity. Scholars and policymakers generally acknowledge that credibility is not about achieving perfection, but about consistent and accountable actions (Eilstrup-Sangiovanni, 2022).

While complete purity in foreign relations might be more of an ideal than a reality, avoiding the appearance of double standards remains crucial for maintaining both trust and influence (Smith, 2021). A practical approach might involve establishing clear and enforceable criteria for arms exports and military cooperation, alongside the rigorous monitoring of human rights conditions (Richards, 2023). This could potentially shift the EU's image from one based on mere rhetoric to one that shows real consequences for abuses, signalling that its values matter, even amidst strategic considerations. Without such steps, the EU risks widening the gap between its stated principles and actual practices, making it more challenging to garner allies or effectively advocate on the global stage (Stahl, 2023).

Case Analysis: EU Responses to Gulf Human Rights Violations

The emphasis placed on values—such as dignity, freedom, and justice—in public statements and policy documents broadly aligns with the EU's human rights commitments. High-level officials frequently express concern about human rights abuses in Gulf countries. This includes political imprisonments, freedom of expression restrictions, and discrimination against women and minorities. There is, however, a noticeable tension. The EU champions human rights, but its dealings with the Gulf often prioritise more pragmatic concerns. Reconciling normative rhetoric with the practical considerations of energy security and regional stability proves difficult [108]. The EU's reliance on Gulf energy supplies and security agreements can render human rights declarations somewhat performative, as business and security interests often seem to dictate policy.

Thus, the EU finds itself in a complex and sometimes contradictory position regarding Gulf rights issues. Official European documents consistently condemn rights violations. Rarely, though, do they advocate for concrete measures that might jeopardise business, such as arms exports or military partnerships. The issue of Germany's arms sales to Riyadh highlights this nicely. Even with disapproval of the Saudi-led war in Yemen and widespread reports of human rights abuses, Germany continues to export weapons, fighter jets and tanks, including to Saudi Arabia. Economic interests or strategic alliances often rationalise this. These transactions exemplify a contradiction in European policy—empty rhetoric about human rights balanced against economic gains and security commitments.

France, similarly, maintains strategic naval bases in the Gulf region, especially in the United Arab Emirates. This signals a long-term security relationship that may undermine efforts to exert pressure on Gulf nations regarding human rights. Such actions show how EU member states navigate the landscape of normative criticism and pragmatic engagement, often resulting in a double standard [109]. These policies may seem solely driven by national interests; however, they also underscore a systemic challenge within EU diplomacy—balancing human rights and multilateral principles against economic dependencies and security concerns.

The Gulf region's importance as a significant portion of Europe's energy supply complicates the EU's ability to take a strong stance against Gulf governments without risking supply disruptions or economic fallout. A military presence, including arms sales and strategic bases, both strengthens security ties and stabilises access to vital energy resources. Many officials openly acknowledge this tension. They might justify arms sales or military cooperation as necessary for regional stability, even though this may conflict with human rights principles.

This complex web of interests often results in reluctance to directly confront Gulf governments, leading to more rhetoric than action in EU responses. Nonetheless, these contradictions have increasingly surfaced in public debates and policy discussions, prompting calls for more consistent and, frankly, courageous approaches. Going forward, the challenge will be whether the EU can reconcile its normative ambitions with the practical realities of regional geopolitics. Perfect consistency is probably unrealistic. The ongoing discourse hinges on whether the EU can integrate human rights into its relationships with Gulf states without, importantly, jeopardising economic or security stability. Policymakers must grapple with these trade-offs. Simultaneously, researchers and advocates analysing specific cases, say, Germany's arms exports or France's military bases, can offer insights into the testing of principles in practice.

10
The Impact of Gulf Realpolitik on EU's Normative Goals

The relationship between the practical politics of the Gulf region and the EU's stated values reveals a notable conflict in international affairs, particularly in terms of supporting democracy and human rights. The EU views itself as a promoter of norms, championing principles such as justice and the rule of law. However, its dealings with Gulf nations often show a pragmatic approach, seemingly prioritising economic gain and regional stability over these principles [110]. The pursuit of secure energy supplies, trade deals, and joint efforts in combating terrorism has led to a transactional strategy.

This approach weakens the EU's capacity to effectively promote its normative framework, as it often requires compromising on its values for strategic gains. Moreover, the EU's mixed feelings about Gulf governments—which tend toward authoritarianism—bring up important questions about the coherence and honesty of its foreign policy [111].

Generally speaking, this situation demonstrates how the compelling realities of Gulf realpolitik sometimes hamper the EU's normative ambitions. This suggests a need to rethink strategies to potentially reconcile these competing needs without giving up fundamental values, generally speaking.

Case Analysis: Arms Trade and Human Rights Contradictions

Germany's arms sales to Saudi Arabia highlight a significant contradiction within the European Union's whole approach

THE EU'S LIMITED LEVERAGE 105

to both human rights and geopolitical strategy. The EU aims to be a champion of human rights and a promoter of peace. However, its actions reveal a more complicated relationship with arms trading, particularly in most cases, in regions where human rights abuses are, sadly, quite prevalent [112]. Saudi Arabia, currently facing criticism for its involvement in the war in Yemen, is both a crucial ally and a buyer of German weaponry. This duality creates, undeniably, a tension, as Germany may inadvertently support a regime that often contradicts the very values the EU claims to uphold.

The German government has explained its arms exports as being based on economic interests and the importance of maintaining strong ties with Gulf nations. Framed to bolster defence partnerships, these arms sales also raise ethical questions. Critics argue that the EU's reliance on Gulf energy and those arms deals compromises its commitment to promoting democracy and human rights in the region [113]. Germany must delicately balance its international responsibilities with the realities of geopolitical alliances. France's decision to establish naval bases in the United Arab Emirates highlights another side of the EU's pragmatic approach to Gulf politics. This move is more than a mere display of military might; it signifies France's commitment to securing its interests in a strategic area.

The UAE, a key regional ally, provides France with a foothold in a volatile region, albeit at a cost. By deepening military ties, France compromises its ability to advocate for human rights and democratic reforms within the UAE, as well as the broader Gulf region. These bases, in a way, serve as a stronghold for French influence, enabling the country to project power and protect its economic interests, particularly in the energy sector. Though France positions itself as a supporter of democratic values, its actions in the region can demonstrate a willingness to disregard authoritarian practices. As with Germany's arms sales, the situation creates a certain disconnect between France's proclaimed values and its strategic decisions. European nations face a real dilemma: how to maintain meaningful relations with Gulf states while upholding their commitments to human rights and multilateralism. Understanding this dynamic is, really, essential for those involved in policymaking and diplomacy. Achieving a healthy relationship with the Gulf while remaining true to foundational European values will require innovative approaches and frank discussions regarding the ethical implications of such strategies. The urgency of addressing these contradictions is paramount for the EU's foreign policy.

Energy Politics and the Erosion of Multilateral Norms

Generally speaking, the intersection of energy politics and weakening multilateral norms poses a considerable hurdle for the European Union's normative goals within the Gulf area. The EU, in most cases, tries to position itself as a normative influence, championing democratic values and human rights. However, the realpolitik that dominates the Gulf states' global interactions arguably limits its reach.

The focus on energy security often prompts EU member states to disregard normative issues in favour of strategic alliances and adopt a pragmatic approach driven by energy dependence demands. This plays out in EU-GCC relations, where shared goals in energy diversification and economic partnership can eclipse core value-based aims [115].

Understanding the dynamics of EU-GCC relations is crucial for policymakers and diplomats, as it can reveal the challenges and opportunities in the region. Thus, the EU's normative structure may face dilution as it navigates the complexities of a multipolar energy landscape, where geopolitical interests often supersede collaborative efforts to uphold international norms. The issues raised by this erosion of multilateral standards underscore the need for the EU to align its normative objectives with the practical realities of Gulf realpolitik, indicating that the balance between moral imperatives and strategic interests is increasingly delicate in energy diplomacy [114].

Energy Politics in Europe

For quite some time, European nations have looked towards the Gulf, with its abundance of oil and gas, to meet their energy demands. Securing a stable energy supply is undoubtedly a key concern, particularly for a continent as reliant on imports as Europe, to keep its lights on and industries running. However, this pursuit of reliable energy can sometimes seem at odds with the EU's stated commitment to human rights and internationally agreed-upon norms.

Take, for example, Germany's arms deals with Saudi Arabia. Berlin often voices support for human rights and cooperation on the world stage. Despite criticism for its human rights record and its involvement in the Yemen conflict, Riyadh continues to receive weapons sales. This tension faced by Germany reflects a larger issue across the European Union. As German weaponry finds its way to Saudi Arabia, advocating for human rights credibly in the Gulf region or elsewhere becomes a difficult task. The financial gains tied to energy imports and arms sales carry more weight than idealistic commitments. This kind of pragmatic policy-making has consequences. Activists and analysts often point out that these arms sales contribute to conflict and hamper peace efforts in Yemen, a humanitarian crisis that the EU claims it wants to resolve [117].

Still, robust economic ties with Riyadh remain, including continued gas imports and lucrative contracts. It raises questions about Europe's normative ambitions when economic dependence affects its willingness to challenge potential abuses by powerful Gulf states. However, the entire Union often finds itself torn between upholding its values and securing the energy supplies its economies require. This complex situation intertwines discussions of multilateral cooperation with energy politics, potentially weakening the EU's global influence. When you have a country selling weapons to an autocracy in the Gulf while also championing human rights at the UN, the disconnect is difficult to ignore.

France, with a slightly different, yet related, approach, reveals another dimension of Gulf-EU relations, where power politics and security intersect. The French Navy's strategic bases in the United Arab Emirates are a beneficial example; they demonstrate how Europe's security interests can sometimes overshadow multilateral principles. These bases help France maintain influence in the region, as well as protect maritime trade routes vital for Europe's energy flow. Having French military assets on Gulf soil suggests a willingness to cooperate with Gulf states beyond just diplomacy and maybe even accepting the political compromises that those relationships entail. The French naval presence in the UAE, in particular, highlights a form of Realpolitik where strategic security may take precedence over full adherence to international norms.

Although the UAE is economically prosperous and strategically important, it faces criticism concerning human rights, labour practices, and military interventions in the region. The fact that France is willing to partner with the Emirates, with a permanent military presence, illustrates how security considerations can sometimes overshadow calls for political reform or accountability on the world stage. Securing energy routes and countering regional instability may take precedence over promoting alignment with international norms. This balancing act reveals the inconsistencies between stated multilateral goals and governmental actions. France quietly projects power in the Gulf, all while navigating the delicate relationship with its sometimes authoritarian partners. Interests that do not always align with Europe's rhetoric shape its foreign policy, as this careful diplomacy demonstrates. As such, the actions taken by European states illustrate a significant transition in India's approach to its foreign policy, moving from normative ideals toward a more realistic framework that acknowledges the complexities of international relations in the current geopolitical landscape [116].

Strategic Compromises and the Future of EU Normative Power

The European Union (EU) aims to champion values—such as transparency, democracy, and human rights—in global affairs. However, France's decisions in the Gulf illustrate a broader European issue: how to reconcile energy security and regional stability with the desire to lead in international law and cooperation [118]. These tensions help explain why the EU can seem fragmented when facing Gulf challenges. The mix of strategic interests, energy needs, and normative ideals yields a nuanced foreign policy, occasionally contradictory and often constrained by competing priorities. Honest questions about these contradictions are vital for an open discussion about Europe's global role. For both researchers and policymakers, spotting the gap between the ideal and the real in EU-Gulf relations is key to developing coherent strategies that resist political and economic pressures. When considering energy politics and multilateral norms, we must remember that every diplomatic choice has consequences that extend beyond immediate gains.

Policies on arms exports, military presence, or energy ties affect perceptions of allies and influence the EU's collective action. A productive approach for the EU might involve transparent mechanisms that openly address these contradictions, encouraging accountability and clearer policies that strike a balance between security needs and human rights considerations. Such a shift could foster greater trust within the Union and internationally, thereby strengthening Europe's credibility and long-term influence in the Gulf. When confronted with Gulf geopolitics, the EU's commitment to human rights, democracy, and multilateral cooperation often encounters significant obstacles.

As a moral standard-bearer, the EU must strike a balance between idealism and practical interests [119]. The Gulf nations, with their energy resources and strategic importance, significantly sway the EU's energy security and diplomacy.

THE EU'S LIMITED LEVERAGE 111

Their presence creates a tug-of-war, leading the EU to make compromises and accept practices it openly criticises, all to maintain influence and trade. These compromises are rarely clear-cut; they weigh the costs of moral dissonance against the benefits of stability or market access. These moments reveal pressure on the EU to prioritise immediate strategic needs over long-term ideals. For instance, policy towards Gulf countries often strikes a balance between criticising authoritarianism and preserving lucrative trade relationships. This tension is particularly evident in high-stakes negotiations, such as arms sales or energy deals, leading to a situation where the EU's moral voice can seem muted. Over time, such exchanges shape perceptions of the EU's moral authority.

As the EU adjusts its position, it raises the question: Is it merely yielding to strategic demands, or is it quietly transforming its identity to pursue influence that is more transactional than normative? Investigating specific instances reveals that Europe's pursuit of principles often conflicts with Realpolitik, as negotiations blur the lines between advocating for rights and safeguarding economic interests. This pattern may result in ethical stands being softened to maintain access or secure energy supplies, ultimately diminishing confidence in the EU's ability to serve as a normative power.

11
Power Dynamics
Comparing EU and Gulf Approaches to Influence

When comparing the EU and the Gulf states, the distinct ways they attempt to exert influence become clear, stemming from very different backgrounds – historical, cultural, and strategic. The EU often promotes democracy, human rights, and the rule of law; however, this 'normative power' doesn't always work well in the Gulf, where matters are more about practical politics. Now, influenced by global events and their focus on resources, the Gulf states impressively use strategic alliances and economic strength to achieve their objectives. As a result, their approaches to the world can be quite different. For example, the EU might push for significant political changes that focus on reform and long-term development.

However, you'll often find that the Gulf countries prefer to use their money and investments immediately to ensure loyalty and expand their global reach. These contrasting foundations make it clear that the EU has limitations in influencing the region, mainly because the Gulf states tend to use strategic moves and various alliances. The varying degrees of influence these entities exert in the world shape their respective roles in international relations, reflecting both normative aspirations and pragmatic realities.

Soft Power vs. Hard Power: Strategies and Outcomes

The European Union has long strived to be a champion of human rights and multilateralism. However, this vision, while idealistic, often bumps against the harsh reality of its substantial dependence on Gulf states for oil and gas – substantial suppliers indeed. Energy security, especially in times of crisis, often takes precedence, making the EU's advocacy of democratic values seem relatively hollow. When the stakes are high, economic interests can overshadow diplomatic aspirations.

This tension becomes evident in the EU's relations with countries such as Saudi Arabia and the UAE. Despite framing its policies around promoting human rights, the EU persists in engaging with regimes that may not necessarily align with these principles. Its reliance on these countries for energy places the EU in a somewhat precarious position. Take Germany, which aspires to leadership in climate policy and human rights; it finds itself negotiating arms deals with Saudi Arabia, raising concerns about its moral standing on the world stage.

Furthermore, multilateralism remains a key part of the EU's ambitions. Initiatives like the Joint Comprehensive Plan of Action with Iran highlight its commitment to diplomacy. Yet, engaging with Gulf nations, the EU's capacity to advocate multilateral solutions often faces hurdles, especially when those nations prioritise security and regional interests over collective action. This seeming inconsistency between the EU's stated goals and its actions leads to questions about the true nature of its soft power and overall effectiveness as a global actor.

In contrast, the Gulf states tend to favour hard power, which refers to the use of military and economical means to influence the behaviour or interests of other political bodies. Significant military expenditures and arms deals evidence this. Countries like Saudi Arabia and the UAE view military capability as a way to enhance regional influence, investing heavily in advanced weaponry and striking deals with Western arms manufacturers. This pragmatic approach enables them to assert influence, circumventing the softer norms that the EU advocates. A striking example of this dynamic surfaces in Germany's decision to pursue arms sales to Riyadh, which has drawn criticism and highlights the complex balancing act between economic and ethical considerations in global relations.

Geopolitical Realities: Military Commerce and Strategic Influence

The recent deal has stirred up a significant quantity of criticism, mainly because it shows a big difference between what Germany says about human rights and what it actually does when it comes to selling weapons. This situation is not unique; it exemplifies the tension between upholding moral principles and safeguarding personal interests in global affairs. A similar trend is evident with India, as it has transitioned from adhering to expectations to embracing a more pragmatic approach [124].

France, meanwhile, has been making its presence felt by establishing naval bases in the UAE. This move is all about strengthening relationships and boosting its strategic position, even though the EU prefers diplomacy and working together. These more assertive strategies show a clear understanding of the current geopolitical situation.

For Gulf countries, maintaining stability and security in a turbulent region often requires a robust military presence. NATO bases and arms deals are viewed as means to demonstrate strength, both domestically and internationally. This strategy is different from the EU's more subtle, behind-the-scenes approach, as discussed in the context of the India-EU partnership [125]. Trying to promote human rights in a region where military power is so significant creates a complex picture of what is happening in the world right now.

The Role of Economic Leverage and Diplomatic engagement

The European Union generally positions itself as a staunch advocate for human rights and a key proponent of multilateral cooperation. It seeks to influence global standards through its considerable economic power, pushing for open markets and adherence to international regulations. Trade agreements act as a significant instrument in this endeavour, linking market access with demands for reforms within partner nations [126]. This image, however, often encounters the harsh realities of international relations, particularly in its interactions with the Gulf states.

The Gulf region's abundant energy resources, which are crucial to European economies, complicate the pursuit of human rights, necessitating a careful balancing act with energy security concerns. European diplomacy, therefore, finds itself navigating between promoting ethical governance and the need to maintain essential oil and gas supplies. We observe this conflict when trade policies or the enforcement of sanctions got eased or postponed due to energy needs, revealing how the EU's declared commitment to multilateralism and human dignity can, at times, appear somewhat superficial when weighed against energy import deals that grant Gulf states substantial economic influence [127].

These imports have an impact not only on economic structures but also on the direction of policymaking, influencing how Europe engages with autocratic regimes. Given this complicated relationship between values and strategic interests, the EU sometimes adopts a somewhat ambiguous stance—supporting human rights while also maintaining close energy and trade ties.

Contrary to the EU's value-based approach, several Gulf states adopt a more pragmatic approach to their international interactions, heavily utilising economic and military ties to expand their influence. Their wealth, derived from oil and gas exports, supports investment in crucial global industries and the funding of advanced arms and military infrastructure. This pragmatic approach prioritises security and influence, often setting aside values and norms that the EU promotes. An illustrative example can be seen in Germany's continued arms sales to Riyadh, which go on despite intense criticism of Saudi Arabia's human rights record, demonstrating a readiness to exchange ethical concerns for economic or geopolitical benefits. Similarly, France demonstrates another aspect of this pragmatic engagement by maintaining military bases in the United Arab Emirates. These presences serve not only as a defence measure but also as signals of a strategic alliance and influence in a turbulent region, thus helping ensure strategic interests and assisting in diplomatic negotiations, while also bolstering France's economic endeavours.

Normative Ambitions vs. Realpolitik in EU-Gulf Relations

EU-Gulf relations are riddled with contradictions, especially when you consider the push and pull between values and vested interests. Spotting these contradictions is key to understanding the difficulties of realistic diplomacy. It is a dance where both sides – the EU and the Gulf states – use their economic muscles to forge strategic alliances, each with its own game plan. A solid grasp of these differing perspectives can help shape policies that take power dynamics into account, pushing for progress incrementally instead of aiming for perfect solutions.

The Ukraine conflict is a stark reminder that the EU is shifting towards a more power-centric strategy, adapting to the shifting sands of geopolitics, where, generally speaking, normative power may not hold as much sway [128]. Going forward, it is essential for observers and policymakers to closely monitor how changes in energy markets or global security issues may impact the economic and diplomatic landscape. These shifts could, in most cases, lead to opportunities for more consistent and, indeed, credible engagement in the long run [129].

Case Comparisons: Gulf's Assertiveness vs. EU's Multilateralism

The Gulf states have long sought to project power and independence onto the global stage. Saudi Arabia, in particular, demonstrates this through significant arms purchases, indicating its desire to wield strategic leverage and influence [Kinninmont, 2018]. These arms deals are not just about modernising military capabilities; they are also messages—messages directed towards both nearby countries and bigger global actors. Riyadh aims to be a central figure in the region [Baqir, 2020]. The United Arab Emirates, meanwhile, has been actively establishing military outposts in key strategic locations, setting up bases and forming partnerships to expand its regional influence [Hoffman, 2021]. Such actions show a clear strategy to appear self-assured, autonomous, and capable of protecting its interests with less reliance on outside help [Feldman, 2019].

This approach to strategic sovereignty marks a shift from traditional diplomacy, which tends to focus on discussion and negotiation between nations [Gordon, 2020]. The Gulf's foreign policy, in contrast, often involves more direct, sometimes even confrontational, methods. For instance, Saudi Arabia has proven its readiness to employ military force when it perceives a threat to its national interests [Laciner, 2018]. This assertiveness also plays out in regional conflicts, where these states support various factions and maintain a strong defence presence [Al-Mansour, 2022]. This all suggests an effort to define their role in global affairs on their own terms, often sidelining international pressures or norms that promote peaceful resolutions and dialogue [Friedman, 2021].

On the other hand, the European Union emphasises multilateralism—an approach focused on cooperation, shared values, and discussion [Mastanduno, 2017]. The EU often presents itself as a champion of human rights and peaceful problem-solving, attempting to resolve issues through dialogue and international bodies [Smith, 2020]. Nevertheless, beneath these ideals, a complicated reality exists. The EU's reliance on oil and gas from the Gulf creates a situation where, depending on energy from countries whose policies it criticises, it can hamper its ability to act decisively [Bennett, 2022].

Take Germany's arms sales to Saudi Arabia, for example. This has sparked debate within the EU about striking a balance between economic benefits and ethical considerations [Bernhardt, 2021]. Similarly, France maintains military bases and naval facilities in Gulf countries such as the UAE, using them as strategic locations to protect European interests in the region [Venturi, 2019]. These bases provide practical support for operations and intelligence gathering, but they also highlight how security and economic considerations can sometimes overshadow the EU's stated dedication to human rights [Zarakhovich, 2018]. It appears that the EU's multilateral approach is becoming increasingly vulnerable due to its dependencies; some critics argue that while the EU promotes international standards, it often compromises them in pursuit of energy security and lucrative defence deals [Bordes, 2023].

The Tension Between Ideals and Interests in EU–Gulf Relations

The EU's diplomatic interactions in the Gulf often reveal a push and pull between its core values and practical necessities, showcasing a delicate dance between its declared principles and strategic actions [132]. While the EU strives to encourage open communication, compliance with global legal standards, and the protection of fundamental human rights, it also participates in arms trading and forms alliances that sometimes necessitate compromising its ideals. For example, Germany's arms exports to Riyadh exemplify this dual approach—while advocating for reform and human rights, Germany also supplies weaponry that risks fuelling regional conflicts [133].

The construction of French military outposts further illustrates a readiness to maintain strategic ties, frequently overlooking ethical considerations that clash directly with EU guidelines. Comprehending these contrasting approaches is key to understanding state power projection. The self-assurance shown by Gulf nations signals both confidence and autonomy, yet it raises potential risks to regional equilibrium if not managed well. At the same time, the EU's dedication to multilateral cooperation aims to foster a stable environment; however, it faces the persistent challenge of aligning its moral principles with the urgent need for energy resources and geopolitical security. Identifying the driving factors behind this interplay helps elucidate why long-held ideals at times stand in opposition to strategic practicalities on the global stage.

Practical Strategies for the EU to Enhance Normative Leverage in the Gulf

For the European Union to truly enhance its influence in the Gulf, a strategic approach is needed – one that combines diplomatic efforts, economic incentives, and cultural exchanges. This would mean a more joined-up foreign policy. Initially, the EU should concentrate on forming robust partnerships with individual countries, prioritising shared values. The EU should prioritise issues such as human rights and the functioning of governments, while always considering the unique circumstances of each Gulf state. After all, the EU has consistently demonstrated an unwavering commitment to its values, as evident in its previous work in the Mediterranean [134].

Also, the EU should use the fact that both regions rely on each other economically. They could offer special trade deals that benefit EU countries, but they could also provide Gulf states with a reason to adopt EU standards for governance and labour practices. It could establish a system where trade benefits are tied to improved human rights records. This way, the EU promotes its values while maintaining friendly relations with the Gulf governments [135].

Lastly, consider enhancing cultural diplomacy. Increase the number of student exchanges and collaborate on art projects to foster better communication and mutual understanding. It is a gentler way to support the EU's values. By consolidating these elements, the EU can gradually establish a robust foundation for its influence, thereby challenging the traditional power dynamics in the Gulf. These changes would make it a more effective global player, one that stands for something.

12
Practical Strategies For the EU to Enhance Normative Leverage

Aligning Energy Policies with Ethical and Human Rights Standards

The European Union has long championed human rights, advocating for individual dignity, liberties, and well-being globally, a moral framework at the heart of its political identity. However, the situation is, in most cases, more intricate. The EU's reliance on energy imports from Gulf states has generally raised questions, especially considering that countries like Saudi Arabia, with their well-documented human rights issues, present a notable contradiction to the EU's ideals [137].

Germany's arms supply to Riyadh, notably, highlights this tension, showcasing a struggle between commercial interests and ethical obligations. The arms trade fuels conflicts that violate human rights while also contributing to the EU's energy security—prompting a serious moral dilemma. This paradox does not merely show moral contradictions; it exposes deeper problems within international relations, illustrating that the EU's energy dependence serves as a reminder that human rights narratives, while powerful in theory, often falter in practice due to geopolitical realities [136].

This reliance on Gulf energy complicates the EU's position, limits its ability to enforce human rights norms, and somewhat weakens its position as a normative power. The EU consequently finds itself at a crossroads, where its practical needs sometimes clash with its human rights aspirations. A fundamental shift in the creation of energy policy is necessary to address this dissonance. For the EU, diversifying energy sources can reduce the reliance on a single region or country. That, in turn, creates leverage when discussing human rights issues.

By investing in renewable energy and fostering partnerships with nations committed to upholding ethical standards, the EU can simultaneously fulfil its human rights commitments and secure reliable energy supplies. This approach requires significant recalibration of relationships and priorities. Beyond diversification, there must be a strong emphasis on responsible procurement. Responsible procurement involves rigorous vetting processes that assess the human rights records of energy suppliers. Such practices aim to ensure that the EU's energy imports do not indirectly fund human rights violations. Moreover, weaving human rights considerations into energy diplomacy transforms the EU's role on the global stage and enhances its credibility as a normative actor in international relations.

Building Strategic Alliances Beyond Energy Dependence

The European Union's efforts to promote human rights and multilateral cooperation often face obstacles, notably its reliance on Gulf energy, which poses a challenge to its moral credibility. The extensive reserves of oil and natural gas controlled by the Gulf Cooperation Council (GCC) countries have become crucial to Europe's economy, creating a dependency that potentially compromises the EU's commitment to its stated values [138]. Discussions about human rights issues or democratic reforms can therefore grow complicated because the boundary separating moral principle and economic advantage becomes unclear, potentially undermining the EU's normative authority and raising questions about potential double standards. An illustrative case is Germany's continued arms sales to Riyadh despite widely known concerns regarding the conflict in Yemen; even as the EU advocates for conflict prevention and democracy, such arms sales ultimately weaken its authority [139].

Likewise, France's military presence in the Gulf, as evidenced by naval bases in the United Arab Emirates, adds another layer to this complex relationship. This presence is partly intended to ensure shared security and stability, positioning France as a close partner to Gulf states rather than solely as a principled external power. Consequently, the European Union, comprising diverse member states and varied aspirations, struggles to reconcile these competing priorities, often resulting in a cautious strategy that limits its ability to make a meaningful difference.

In most cases, the EU's energy ties serve as both a lifeline and a constraint, affording it some influence but simultaneously undercutting the clarity of its message. Suppose the EU wants to expand its influence beyond its current entanglements. In that case, it may be necessary to strengthen partnerships beyond those related to energy, pursuing alliances that prioritise shared objectives in fields such as technology, education, health, and climate policy. By involving Gulf states and other global entities in these areas, the EU can foster trust and mutual respect based on shared advantages rather than pure necessity. Supporting cooperation on alternative energy programs and diversification projects offers an opportunity for both the EU and Gulf states to reduce problematic dependencies. Away from the focus on oil fields and pipelines, there is a potential for collaborative research, cultural exchanges, and strengthened private sector relationships that connect societies in less controversial ways.

EU's Strategic Diversification

The EU might consider backing renewable energy infrastructure projects or implementing education initiatives aimed at enhancing relevant skills. Increased joint work to tackle pressing regional issues — like water shortages or public health emergencies – could also be on the cards [140]. It is essential that the EU keeps its focus on ethics, constantly reminding its partners that respect for human rights and adherence to international law truly matter [141]. One could argue that developing strategic connections beyond the Gulf, involving emerging countries and regional bodies, should mitigate the risks associated with relying too heavily on a single region.

Practically speaking, the argument suggests working more closely with African and Asian nations, as well as deeper cooperation with bodies that champion legal standards and democratic systems. Alliances grounded in both principle and practicality are essential for successfully navigating these hurdles. The EU's future clout hinges on the strength and scope of its relationships, perhaps even more than just energy supply lines. Ideally, the strategy includes establishing platforms for cooperation in areas besides energy, to help transform positive attitudes into firm commitments.

Strategic partnerships in areas such as education, the arts, and sustainable development are crucial if the EU wants to remain a strong advocate for human rights and regulations.

Innovative Diplomatic Tools for Normative Influence

Informal channels, such as Track II diplomacy, are critical—perhaps even crucial—for shaping how countries perceive each other and act, beyond just formal talks. These informal conversations foster understanding and trust, leading to the creation of global norms that garner greater consensus [142]. For instance, cultural exchanges, such as art and academic partnerships, function as effective 'soft power' tools, fostering mutual understanding and cooperation among nations.

The Internet also plays a part; social media allows you to communicate instantly with people all over the world. This means campaigns can fight unfair stereotypes and push what everyone wants. These campaigns have a subtle effect on what the public and policymakers think, which helps everyone address today's foreign policy problems in a more integrated way [143].

Engaging with Gulf Partners: Strategies for Promoting Normative Values

Online campaigns can be powerful tools for governments and civil society, allowing them to promote universal values,

THE EU'S LIMITED LEVERAGE 131

human rights, and open dialogue [144]. Discussions unfolding in real-time on platforms like Twitter and LinkedIn, for instance, can help bridge gaps between Gulf and European audiences, often making complex issues more relatable, generally speaking. Virtual town halls or webinars are also beneficial as they bring together a range of voices, which then fosters ongoing conversations that might be limited otherwise by physical borders. Additionally, digital tools enable targeted messaging based on demographics or region, increasing the likelihood of resonance.

Consider, for example, a series of webinars put together by EU diplomats aimed at young Gulf audiences, where the importance of civil liberties and effective governance [145] was discussed. When these efforts are consistent and systematic, they can gradually establish a culture where certain norms become ingrained in everyday conversation, shaping attitudes over time. The real key is authenticity and, above all, patience—seeking to embed values gently, rather than seeming to impose them.

One route to influence revolves around joint policy initiatives that directly involve Gulf partners and European institutions. These initiatives show a willingness to collaborate on shared interests, such as climate change, counter-terrorism, or trade, in most cases. Designed to include normative goals—like promoting gender equality or human rights—they can subtly encourage Gulf countries to adopt higher standards without feeling coerced. Take, for example, a collaborative environmental project that includes commitments to sustainable development, aligning economic incentives with normative values. Conditionalities can also serve as gentle nudges. Countries that demonstrate progress on specific issues may gain access to resources, support, or preferential agreements. Such incentives aim to motivate reforms while maintaining a cooperative tone.

Multilateral platforms, like regional security or economic forums, are also places where people can work together to strengthen norms. These forums let people from the Gulf and Europe share best practices, hold each other accountable, and build a sense of shared responsibility. Over time, these joint efforts can foster a normative climate rooted in cooperation, rather than dominance. Another important strategy is to set up places where people from the Gulf and Europe can talk to each other on a regular basis, both formally and informally. These spaces bolster the ongoing exchange of ideas, building trust and encouraging normative alignment. For instance, including human rights issues in trade talks or security deals can show how important they are and gently push Gulf partners to deal with sensitive issues over time.

When multilateral platforms are open to civil society participation—such as NGOs, think tanks, or community groups—they add broader voices to the conversation. This diversity can pressure governments to adopt more ethical practices. Practical steps might involve establishing joint working groups or task forces dedicated to specific issues, such as labour standards or anti-corruption initiatives. Such initiatives emphasise shared interests and collective responsibility, reinforcing normative principles in everyday policy practices rather than abstract ideals.

The overall idea is to embed normative influence within the framework of practical cooperation, making it part of the ongoing dialogue rather than an external demand. Fostering transparency and accountability in these initiatives becomes crucial. When Gulf countries see clear benefits and shared gains from aligning with EU norms, such as economic development or regional stability, they tend to become more receptive. It is about creating a sense that normative progress is not just about moral imperatives, but also about practical advantages.

Consistent engagement and positive reinforcement can build a steady influence, shaping norms through adaptation rather than confrontation, generally speaking. Those involved in these processes must remain aware that change usually takes time, and patience remains essential in cultivating lasting normative shifts among diverse partners.

13
Navigating the Tensions
Policy Recommendations and Best Practices

Balancing Commercial Interests with Ethical Commitments

Generally speaking, Europe is continually trying to strike a delicate balance: its human rights ideals versus its pressing energy needs, which are often fulfilled by Gulf nations. Germany's arms sales to Saudi Arabia are an example of this; the EU wants to make its position on human rights and multilateralism clear. However, these aspirations often clash with the responsibilities tied to economic reliance on, particularly, energy imports [146]. Germany, for instance, has maintained a long-standing commitment to human rights, yet its decision to sell arms to Riyadh illustrates the contradiction between these ethical commitments and economic interests [147].

Critics argue these arms may contribute to conflicts that contravene fundamental human rights. Therefore, the question arises: how can European nations profess to champion human rights while actively engaging in trade that might fuel violations?

France's establishment of naval bases in the United Arab Emirates reflects another complex layer. These bases support strategic military partnerships and economic investments in Gulf states. Nevertheless, they raise ethical questions about France's stance on human rights and regional stability. Such networks of bases symbolise the intertwined relationships between security, trade, and ethical governance. It demonstrates that Europe must confront these dilemmas when dealing with Gulf nations. The challenge remains critical: how can countries like Germany and France reconcile their economic dependencies with what constitutes genuine commitments to ethical governance?

Policymakers face the need to find practical solutions that balance trade relations with ethical obligations. Enhancing transparency in arms deals and energy agreements may be one pathway. By creating a clear framework that outlines how transactions benefit both parties while adhering to ethical considerations, Europe can foster trust and accountability when dealing with Gulf nations. Establishing public records and independent oversight bodies can monitor these transactions, ensuring these partnerships do not come at the cost of overlooking human rights violations.

Multilateral engagement may be another means to bridge the gap between ethics and commerce.

The EU can increase its bargaining power by working collectively with other nations. Joint efforts could lead to agreements that prioritise ethical considerations in addition to commercial interests. European leaders, for example, in negotiations with Gulf states, could emphasise collaborative commitments to sustainable development, which would bind both sides to higher human rights standards while addressing energy needs. Strategic diversification of energy sources is crucial, particularly in light of the pressing climate crisis and shifting geopolitical landscapes. The EU could invest more in renewable energy technologies rather than leaning solely on Gulf energy. Fostering relationships with other countries that prioritise environmental sustainability may allow Europe to reduce its dependence on any single region and strengthen its stance on ethical governance. The path forward requires both courage and commitment to change. The reward? A more ethically driven foreign policy that still meets commercial needs is well worth the effort. Policymakers must be bold in taking steps toward a more ethical economic landscape. Engaging in open dialogue about these challenges can spark meaningful change and rebuild trust in Europe's commitment to human rights.

Leveraging Multilateral Institutions for Normative Goals

The European Union relies on multilateral institutions as key arenas for projecting its values, especially when navigating regions where real-world politics do not always align with its ideals. Consider the Gulf, a region renowned for its shifting alliances and intricate security dynamics, which makes it a particularly challenging environment. The EU champions principles such as human rights and democracy, but these ideals often clash with the practical considerations that shape Gulf relations. Through bodies like the UN or the World Trade Organisation, the EU seeks to push its agenda through diplomacy and negotiation. Gulf states, however, view these institutions with a more pragmatic eye: they offer international legitimacy, economic opportunities, and security assurances. The EU's goals have a better chance of gaining traction if presented as shared aims rather than externally imposed ideals. Generally speaking, Gulf governments tend to favour bilateral deals and seek tighter control. While multilateral platforms aim to distribute influence more broadly, the EU sometimes receives scepticism from Gulf states, which are wary of external pressure on sensitive internal issues.

Consider, for example, Germany's ongoing arms sales to Saudi Arabia. This exemplifies the occasional tension between human rights rhetoric and economic imperatives. Such inconsistencies might erode the EU's credibility in international discussions. Conversely, France's naval presence in the UAE illustrates how military engagement and diplomatic influence can intersect, affording France leverage in discussions about governance and regional security. It shows how normative ambitions and Realpolitik can coexist, albeit sometimes uneasily. The EU can strengthen its position by connecting its moral goals to real-world issues, such as fighting terrorism and keeping the region stable. That is, framing human rights not just as moral requirements, but as essential for lasting cooperation.

The EU-Gulf relationship frequently requires striking a balance between the EU's commitment to promoting human rights and the need for stable energy. Navigating this tricky terrain requires more than just rhetoric; it calls for strategies that deliver tangible, mutual benefits. Within international organisations, the EU can build alliances with Gulf nations based on shared interests, such as climate change and infrastructure investments. By focusing on mutual objectives, the EU can gradually introduce broader discussions on governance and accountability. This approach requires flexibility, given the EU's reliance on Gulf energy; oil and gas remain vital, especially in light of broader geopolitical tensions. Instead of demanding immediate policy changes, the EU could leverage these forums to push for gradual social reforms that promote transparency and labour rights, especially in energy-related sectors.

Furthermore, initiatives involve knowledge sharing, supporting Gulf sustainability efforts, and emphasising the human rights aspects of environmental policies. Specific examples reveal this careful choreography. Germany's arms sales to Riyadh, despite public criticism, show how economic interests can sometimes overshadow human rights concerns. However, without ongoing dialogue, progress can stall. France's military presence in the UAE, meanwhile, shows how soft power can translate influence into policy. Therefore, the EU may benefit from increasing its investments in cultural diplomacy and technical partnerships, fostering more profound engagement and promoting both economic and democratic advancements.

EU Relations with Gulf States: Finding a Balance Between Interests and Morals

Multilateral institutions provide platforms to foster the trust necessary for productive dialogue, which in turn enables more open discussions on rights and freedoms. Shared concerns for prosperity and security frame these conversations. Rather than pushing for broad reforms immediately, an incremental approach can be more effective; the EU might focus on more minor, significant improvements that build credibility with Gulf partners. For example, the EU could support Gulf participation in UN human rights initiatives or endorse collaborative research on shared regional issues. While these are modest steps, they can establish a foundation for change without confrontation. A norm-based relationship can develop over time, integrating EU ideals into a practical agenda rather than presenting them as an unattainable benchmark.

Balancing principle with pragmatism, patience, and persistence is therefore key [150]. The EU can act through both governmental and non-governmental channels, uniting diplomats, civil society figures, business leaders, and academics. These combined perspectives, within multilateral institutions, can enrich discussions and broaden the possibilities for reconciling Gulf interests with European values. Greater credibility—achieved when engagement acknowledges the realities of the region—helps narrow the gap between rhetoric and reality [151]. For both researchers and policymakers, it is essential to view multilateral institutions not just as ideological battlegrounds, but as arenas for dialogue, compromise, and problem-solving that can gradually shape international norms. Understanding the interplay between Gulf Realpolitik and EU normative objectives is essential for developing approaches that transcend mere pronouncements. The objective is often less about winning a single point and more about developing an enduring cooperative structure that can weather geopolitical shifts.

Designing Incentives and Sanctions to Promote Human Rights

The European Union navigates a challenging landscape in its dealings with Gulf nations. A significant portion of the region's economic strength stems from exporting oil and gas, the cornerstone of their economies [152]. These resources are vitally important to the EU, representing a critical piece of its energy strategy, particularly as it aims to lessen its dependency on Russian energy. However, the relationship creates a tacit understanding. This energy imperative frequently tests the EU's public commitment to human rights and democratic principles. While nations such as Saudi Arabia and the UAE have faced international criticism for their human rights records, the EU often prioritises maintaining energy supplies, resulting in a tangled mix of dependency and diplomatic manoeuvring. This reliance forces the EU into a careful game of incentives and deterrents.

Diplomatic pressure, including public pronouncements and careful negotiation, is used to encourage reforms in Gulf states in a subtle manner; however, such discussions are often complicated by economic factors. Reducing energy imports or reassessing trade agreements could potentially disrupt supply chains and damage European economies. Germany's arms sales to Riyadh, for example, highlight this tension.

Though EU members officially express concern regarding the conflict in Yemen and human rights violations, military equipment sales continue, reflecting a compromise between ethical considerations and economic realities [153]. Similarly, France's naval presence in the Gulf enhances strategic influence, yet these connections could, in some instances, weaken the ability to advocate for democratic change. It is also important to note that, while these nations exert considerable influence over the EU's energy security, putting pressure on human rights could potentially backfire, which would destabilise supply stability and economic interests.

Balancing Economic Interests and Human Rights in EU-Gulf Relations

The unresponsiveness of Gulf countries to diplomatic threats affecting their core interests further complicates matters. Their political structures tend to be less sensitive to external pressures, particularly when significant economic advantages are at stake. When the EU advocates for improvements in human rights or governance, Gulf governments often resist, describing such demands as undue external interference [154]. This back-and-forth dynamic restricts the EU's influence, forcing it to balance promoting its values with acknowledging economic reliance.

Many European policymakers understand that simply increasing the volume of their demands will not immediately alter the deep-rooted regional dynamics. Instead, they are looking into more subtle strategies that take into account the realities of geopolitics, such as combining incentives with more nuanced diplomatic efforts [155]. This balancing act, inherently contradictory, has become a hallmark of contemporary EU-Gulf relations.

Given these challenges, the EU must formulate policies that navigate the tension between economic dependence and the aspiration to advance human rights. Targeted sanctions provide a precise tool for application. Rather than employing broad economic measures, policies could single out specific actors—for example, individuals implicated in rights violations or entities participating in arms deals that exacerbate conflicts. This method reduces unintended harm while conveying distinct messages. For instance, freezing assets or restricting travel to designated officials can prove effective without destabilising entire economies.

In parallel with sanctions, the EU might develop strategic incentives that reward constructive actions. Providing trade advantages or investment opportunities to Gulf countries through transparent agreements linked to tangible reforms can stimulate gradual progress. Diplomacy also requires greater sophistication. Instead of generalised condemnations, engaging in discreet, sustained dialogue is often more effective.

Cultivating trust facilitates incremental advancements. For example, European nations might provide technical support for governance reform initiatives or conduct joint discussions on regional stability, integrating human rights into a broader framework of cooperation. Moreover, multilayered diplomacy, which involves not only governments but also business leaders, civil society organisations, and regional bodies, creates a broader network of influence.

This approach acknowledges the interconnectedness of economic relations and political commitments. This approach can foster an environment that not only requests reform but also provides tangible rewards. Employing such pragmatic tools could pave the way for the EU to promote universal values without jeopardising vital economic interests. Ultimately, striking a balance involves aligning incentives with regional geopolitical realities. The EU cannot simply eliminate Gulf energy supplies overnight without severe consequences.

However, it can design comprehensive policy packages that gradually transition the relationship from one based purely on transactions to one based on greater cooperation, founded on shared values. Encouraging Gulf countries

THE EU'S LIMITED LEVERAGE 145

to recognise how respecting human rights can also bolster their long-term stability and prosperity can make a difference. Setting clear benchmarks linked to specific reforms, while maintaining open communication channels, sustains the dialogue and keeps it productive. It is not about imposing uniform solutions but about translating shared interests into concrete, achievable steps – a process that, although perhaps slower, lays the groundwork for lasting progress over time.

14
Future Outlook
The Evolution of EU-Gulf Relations

Looking ahead, the development of relations between the EU and the Gulf region involves a complicated interaction. It is a mix between what the EU hopes for normatively and what is actually happening in Gulf politics. The Gulf Cooperation Council (GCC) countries are keen on security, diversifying their economies, and increasing their influence in the region. As a result, they have been working more closely with various major global powers, such as China and Russia. This engagement with multiple centres of power challenges the EU's longstanding role as a promoter of democratic values and human rights. These values sometimes seem at odds with the authoritarian governments in the Gulf.

However, the EU's commitment to fostering economic ties through initiatives such as the European Union-Gulf Cooperation Council Free Trade Agreement could serve as a valuable foundation for discussion. It could enable the EU to use its economic power to address shared concerns about stability and climate change. Future interactions will necessitate the EU's practical adjustment of its normative framework. That would mean aligning its diplomatic efforts with the actual geopolitical situation in the Gulf, which would help create a stronger partnership that balances what each side wants with shared values. This development will be crucial in shaping the EU's role as a significant player in the complex geopolitical landscape of the Gulf.

Emerging Trends: Renewable Energy, Tech, and Security Cooperation

Renewable energy projects, new technologies, and shared security concerns are increasingly shaping EU-Gulf relations. This convergence underscores the complex relationship between the objectives of both parties and the practical realities of global politics. With Gulf Cooperation Council (GCC) members putting more emphasis on diversifying their energy sources—partly due to the unstable nature of fossil fuel markets and growing climate concerns—the EU can offer valuable strategic partnerships, given its experience in sustainability. It is not just about environmental necessity, though; the booming tech industry also plays a significant role, particularly in innovative grid development and energy efficiency-promoting technologies.

Moreover, energy security and security cooperation are becoming more intertwined as both regions face similar threats, such as those from non-state actors, and vulnerabilities in their energy infrastructure related to cybersecurity. Thus, even as the EU seeks to use its influence to promote sustainable development, it must carefully consider the practical aspects of Gulf Realpolitik, where immediate national interests often supersede long-term normative goals. This situation makes it crucial to understand how new developments in renewable energy and technology can either foster cooperation or become a point of contention, contingent on whether strategic interests align.

Renewable Energy and EU-Gulf Cooperation

Renewable energy and associated technologies are redefining the relationship between the EU and Gulf nations. The Gulf region, historically a key player in fossil fuel markets—supplying Europe with energy while benefiting from Western technology—now faces a shifting global landscape favoured by cleaner energy sources. Discussions on public health governance highlight the structural adjustments needed for energy policy transitions [160]. This evolution opens up avenues for Gulf states to diversify their economies, reducing their reliance on oil, as the EU aims to bolster its energy security and reduce its carbon footprint. Gulf countries are increasingly investing in renewable infrastructure; solar and wind projects are central to national sustainability strategies.

For instance, Saudi Arabia's Vision 2030 features ambitious plans for renewable energy generation, indicating a willingness to consider alternatives to traditional energy exports. The EU sees this as a chance to strengthen partnerships and create technologies that will help with its Green Deal and climate goals. Technological advancements, such as those in energy storage and smart grids, are also transforming this collaboration. The EU's expertise in these areas offers potential for knowledge sharing and joint projects. European firms might collaborate with Gulf states on solar farms or hydrogen production, shifting the focus from energy imports to collaborative energy transition.

Geopolitics significantly impacts security cooperation between the EU and Gulf states, as both entities navigate complex relationships shaped by historical ties, economic interests, and security concerns. European nations, Germany and France, have significant security interests in the Gulf. However, tensions exist between promoting human rights and relying on energy imports from countries with questionable human rights records.

For example, Germany's arms sales to Riyadh, despite concerns over human rights abuses in Yemen, reflect how economic interests can take precedence. This situation raises questions about the EU's commitment to its values. France's naval bases in the UAE highlight its security ties, potentially indicating a preference for strategic partnerships over normative goals. These factors present a challenging balance for both parties.

For policymakers and analysts in EU-Gulf relations, staying informed is vital. Understanding the link between energy transitions and security dynamics can foster productive discussions, especially considering strategic analyses of defence policy [161]. As the EU and Gulf states pursue their objectives, dialogue and understanding are crucial for fostering trust and addressing everyday challenges. Strengthening this cooperation is not just strategic but also an opportunity for growth in a changing world. A practical approach should emphasise mutual benefits, respect governmental structures, and pursue shared goals, leading to a sustainable and secure future for both regions.

Potential Shifts in Gulf Strategies and EU Responses

The Gulf's evolution has triggered fresh assessments of regional tactics and the EU's response plans, mainly because new geopolitical partnerships are disrupting the old power structures. Gulf nations are expanding their economic ties and increasing their global presence. The EU is encountering obstacles when exercising its normative power. Historically, this power depended on diplomatic efforts built on shared values and legal structures [162].

This switch highlights a growing tendency for Gulf states to adopt a Realpolitik approach, where what works often trumps ideological harmony. This, in turn, complicates the EU's ability to shape regional stability and governance. The EU's reliance on normative power theory—promoting human rights and democratic values as key components of its foreign policy—needs to adapt slightly to accommodate these new realities [163].

These different approaches to doing things highlight the extent to which the EU can actually influence developments in a rapidly changing geopolitical world. It also advocates for a strategic rethink, one that acknowledges the complexity of Gulf politics and the necessity of pragmatic engagement, rather than relying on hope.

Gulf States' Evolving Strategies

Across the Gulf, states are rethinking their strategies, primarily driven by the shifting geopolitical landscape in the Middle East and beyond. Studies have highlighted how the established role these nations hold, particularly as energy suppliers, is undergoing significant changes. Now, the push is on to reduce dependence on oil and diversify the economy

[164].

Consider the United Arab Emirates and Saudi Arabia; they are investing substantial funds in technology, tourism, and finance, aiming for economic strength that extends beyond oil and gas. At the same time, you cannot ignore security. Security continues to be a crucial component. Tensions are up in the Gulf region, considering Iran's growing reach in the area and the tricky situations playing out in places like Yemen and Syria.

These governments must juggle protecting their own territory with maintaining stability at home and demonstrating strength on the global stage. While seeking new allies and acting more independently, they are careful not to rely too heavily on any single outside power. It is a delicate balancing act involving the United States, China, Russia, and various regional players [165].

European Union and Gulf Dynamics

For the European Union, the evolving landscape in the Gulf region presents both opportunities and challenges. Brussels, generally speaking, has long championed a foreign policy rooted in values, placing significant emphasis on multilateral cooperation, human rights, and democracy. However, these ideals often find themselves at odds with economic and geopolitical interests when considering the Gulf states, particularly given the EU's substantial reliance on Gulf energy imports. Taking a firm stance on human rights or political matters becomes challenging due to this dependency. Consider, for example, the controversies surrounding Germany's arms sales to Riyadh, despite concerns regarding the conflict in Yemen; these episodes further highlight contradictions apparent in European foreign policy [166].

Meanwhile, France appears to favour a more pragmatic approach, maintaining naval bases in the United Arab Emirates to safeguard its strategic interests and protect vital trade routes. This blend of values-driven diplomacy and Realpolitik highlights the EU's challenge in developing a coherent position in the region. Some member states champion normative diplomacy, while others prioritise business ties and security, limiting Brussels' capacity for unified action. As Gulf states display growing geopolitical confidence, the EU faces increasing pressure to reassess its approach to upholding its principles without sacrificing influence or access. Reconciling its role as a promoter of human rights with the reality of economic and security dependency on the Gulf represents one of the EU's critical dilemmas.

The tightening control of Gulf states over political expression and civil society contrasts sharply with the EU's commitment to openness and inclusion. However, enforcing these ideals too rigidly risks alienating Gulf partners, who play crucial roles in energy markets and regional stability. Efforts, such as joint investments in renewable energy or defence cooperation, to build strategic resilience in the Gulf provide potential pathways to balance these competing interests. For instance, European firms are increasingly involved in green energy projects in the Gulf, which might nurture a more constructive relationship.

The EU may also advocate for incremental improvements in labour rights and governance by aligning dialogue with economic incentives rather than resorting to confrontation. Navigating this intricate landscape demands both patience and nuance, particularly as Gulf countries become more adept at managing foreign influence and pursuing their ambitions. Consider, for instance, Germany's ongoing weapons exports to Saudi Arabia, which exemplify the tensions inherent in these dynamics. Despite public criticism and calls from human rights organisations, German firms continue to supply arms potentially used in Yemen's conflict, sparking a debate about balancing economic interests and moral responsibility.

Conversely, France's military presence in the Gulf, including naval bases in the UAE, reflects a different style of engagement, that emphasises security cooperation and a more traditional balance-of-power approach. These divergent strategies reveal fissures in the EU's unified posture, demonstrating how national priorities frequently take precedence over collective EU policies, especially when critical security considerations and lucrative contracts are at stake [167]. This fragmentation consequently limits the EU's ability to influence the Gulf cohesively and undermines its authority when advocating for reforms.

Gulf Strategies and EU Relations

The EU, facing the Gulf's evolving approach, arguably needs a revised strategy for projecting influence. More honest dialogues may emerge from improved engagement frameworks that incorporate economic, security, and human rights elements [169]. Constructive engagement also involves supporting regional conflict resolution initiatives and investing in development projects spearheaded by the Gulf. However, it is important to acknowledge limitations; normative arguments alone will likely be insufficient, particularly with options like China and Russia available.

Therefore, a balanced approach—pragmatic yet principled—could prove more effective, combining engagement with clear communication on rights and governance. Reinforcing existing collaborations in areas of shared concern, such as climate change and the energy transition, might be one such practical step. These joint efforts can foster trust and create avenues for broader cooperation, given the shared pressures of reducing emissions and adapting to future economic challenges.

Concurrently, Brussels could strive to bolster the EU's strategic independence by lessening energy dependence. Diversifying energy sources and investing in European renewables would give the EU more agency to engage with the Gulf, moving beyond mere necessity [168]. Crucially, understanding the Gulf's geopolitical dexterity is vital; these nations skilfully navigate competing interests, benefiting from multiple powers without total commitment. Thus, the EU's approach must be subtle, offering dialogue and incentives without driving the Gulf toward rivals such as Beijing or Washington. Patience, flexibility, and accepting incremental progress may characterise the future of this energy-, security-, and value-laden relationship.

Long-Term Scenarios for Normative Power and Realpolitik Interplay

A rather complex situation arises from the European Union's,

THE EU'S LIMITED LEVERAGE 157

shall we say, *ambition* to set a moral standard, especially when juxtaposed with the Gulf states' more pragmatic leanings [Smith, 2020]. The EU has, over time, consistently championed human rights, environmental concerns, and multilateralism. This advocacy, however, has not always aligned smoothly with Gulf countries, who tend to prioritise regional stability and, of course, energy security [Jones, 2021]. Looking ahead, such differences might become even *more* noticeable. This could prompt the EU to intensify its normative policies, even in the face of resistance [Brown, 2022]. Consider Germany; they might continue selling arms to Saudi Arabia, explaining it as a matter of strategy and the economy, despite valid criticism regarding human rights [Miller, 2023].

In contrast, the Gulf states' heavy reliance on energy exports, along with their established alliances, often runs counter to the EU's efforts to promote political changes or democratic ideals [Williams2020]. What could happen in the future? Well, there are a few possible scenarios. For instance, maybe things will gradually smooth out, and economic ties and shared interests could soften some of those sharp divides. Gulf countries, as they attempt to diversify away from oil, may be more receptive to diplomatic pressure on issues such as human rights or climate policy [Khan, 2021].

However, there is also a real possibility that things will drift further apart. Gulf states could strengthen their independence, viewing EU standards as unwelcome interference [Ali, 2023]. This could then create more isolated regional groups, less open to EU influence and more focused on their own ideas of stability and progress. These kinds of divisions could potentially influence global alliances for many years and shape how normative ideas and practical interests mix or clash [Taylor, 2022]. Whether this relationship remains balanced ultimately hinges on how each side defines its own goals.

15
Conclusion
Reassessing the EU's Normative Power in a Realpolitik World

This investigation into the European Union's normative power, when viewed in the context of the Gulf region, leads us to a deeper understanding of how ideals and real-world practicalities interact. Generally speaking, the EU puts forward a normative vision—a structure built around the idea of spreading democratic values and championing human rights. However, its effectiveness often suffers due to the realpolitik—the practical politics—that influences relationships in the Gulf. This tension between the EU's intended normative goals and the established interests of important actors in the region presents considerable difficulties with its influence.

Several scholars have pointed out that this very strain represents a wider strategic problem for the EU in its various foreign policy efforts, specifically as the EU attempts to navigate a world increasingly shaped by power politics and the interests of individual states [172]. It seems a recalibration is needed; one that understands the limits of normative power in situations where economic and security concerns are paramount. Recent ideas from within the English School of International Relations emphasise the importance of initiating a more nuanced discussion, one that reconciles the EU's core principles with the harsh realities of geopolitical positioning [173]. This nuanced discussion can stimulate intellectual engagement and lead to more effective foreign policy decisions.

Synthesising Lessons from Case Studies and Strategic Analyses

The European Union often portrays itself as a strong supporter of human rights and a partner to other countries. However, its reliance on energy from the Gulf region raises an intriguing conflict. While EU leaders discuss a world based on fairness and equality, things are not so simple [174]. The EU relies on energy from Gulf countries to sustain its economy, which can create tension between its principles and its practical needs. The issue becomes particularly evident when examining how some Gulf countries approach human rights. Often, the EU says one thing but does another because it prioritises securing energy over upholding beneficial governance and freedoms. This aspect not only raises questions about ethics but also makes people wonder if the EU is trustworthy on the world stage. Maintaining a steady energy supply often takes precedence over the goal of promoting democratic ideals. In a world driven by practical politics, the EU's voice is not as loud on important human rights issues [175].

As a result, a gap exists between the EU's values and its practical interests.

Many people wonder if its foreign policy can ever truly match the principles it claims to have. For instance, Germany's selling weapons to Saudi Arabia shows how Europe is ready to compromise its stated values for the sake of real-world politics. Even though people are worried about how Saudi Arabia treats its citizens and its actions in Yemen, Germany keeps selling military equipment to them. This reveals a concerning trend: economic benefits often outweigh ethical concerns. Selling weapons contradicts the moral stance that the EU claims to support. Additionally, it highlights how countries' economic ties can affect their political choices, often at the expense of fairness and human rights.

Similarly, France's establishment of naval bases in the UAE demonstrates the compromises necessary for important security relationships. These bases are crucial for France to maintain its military influence in the Gulf, enabling it to demonstrate its power and contribute to regional security. Still, this military cooperation means that France and the EU must be cautious when criticising their partners' human rights records. Depending on military and economic connections can create a complex situation where strategic interests take precedence over human rights.

These examples reveal a significant problem: how can the EU genuinely support human rights when it is so closely tied to partners who may not share those values? Finding the right approach to this is a tricky balancing act, and it often fails. Generally speaking, it often appears to falter due to the complexities involved.

Navigating Values and Strategic Interests in the EU's Foreign Policy

Looking at the challenges in the real world, it becomes clear that advocates and scholars have a vital role to play. They need to push for transparency and accountability, especially when it comes to partnerships involving energy and defence.

As Levy pointed out in 2015, effective advocacy can really make a difference, steering policy changes by getting people more involved and demanding more oversight. The EU could start to close the gap between what it says it values and what it actually does in foreign policy, demanding a more transparent alignment.

Recent studies, like the one by Smith in 2020, highlight how inconsistencies in EU policy can hurt its reputation worldwide. This alignment is crucial; it fosters trust not only among EU members but also with countries outside the EU, thereby reinforcing its image as a trustworthy player on the global stage (Jones, 2018). By empowering advocates and scholars, the EU can ensure that its foreign policy decisions are informed by a diverse range of perspectives, making them more effective and credible.

Identifying Pathways for a More Effective and Credible EU Role

Often, the European Union presents itself as a champion of democracy, international law, and human rights, projecting an image of peaceful global cooperation (European Union, 2020). However, this image frequently contrasts with its energy demands, particularly in the Gulf region. The EU's reliance on oil and gas from Gulf states, such as Qatar, the UAE, and Saudi Arabia, strains its moral position (Santos, 2022).

Although Brussels promotes multilateralism and often criticises human rights issues, its member states sustain economic relationships that sometimes contradict these principles. For example, Germany's ongoing arms sales to Riyadh, despite criticism over Yemen (Klein, 2021), or France's naval presence in the UAE, which suggests support for Gulf governments both militarily and diplomatically (Le Roux, 2021), highlight this contradiction. These examples have a significant impact on the EU's international perception. On the one hand, Brussels advocates for robust human rights standards (Smith, 2019), while on the other, it relies on Gulf energy to meet its economic needs, particularly given the slow and uneven transition away from fossil fuels (Zahra, 2023).

This reliance forces the EU to balance carefully; intense public criticism of rights abuses risks jeopardising energy security (Olsen, 2022). This tension weakens the EU's credibility with its Gulf partners, who view its moral stance sceptically (Hansen, 2021). In response, Gulf states use their energy exports to influence dialogue, thereby softening EU pressure and integrating interests with values (Bennett, 2020). Energy security is vital for Europe's functioning, especially during geopolitical instability (Meyer, 2021), pushing many EU countries to maintain ties with regimes that starkly differ in governance from the EU's values.

This clash between normative goals and geopolitical needs creates a gap that can be exploited (Fischer, 2021), leading to confusion among EU audiences and policymakers about where to draw the lines. It also complicates alliances within the EU, as some members favour rigid stances while others prioritise energy supplies and economic ties (Schmidt, 2022). Germany, with its robust industry and reliance on Gulf hydrocarbons, contrasts with France's approach, which combines security cooperation with diplomatic initiatives (Bradley, 2023).

The EU's credibility hinges on striking a balance between its values and its strategic interests in the Gulf (Giovannetti, 2022). To achieve this, honesty about limitations is crucial. Instead of adhering to a purely moral approach or succumbing to pragmatism, the EU might consider adopting hybrid strategies (Kim, 2023). This involves engaging Gulf partners with clear expectations of human rights, while also seeking diverse energy sources and promoting cleaner alternatives (Baker, 2023). Pragmatism need not mean abandoning principles, but instead embracing flexible, context-sensitive diplomacy that builds trust through transparency (Vasquez, 2022).

The EU's Strategic Engagement with the Gulf: Balancing Values and Interests

To illustrate, EU nations might strengthen efforts to link energy partnerships to tangible improvements in human rights standards. Policy design should reward progress instead of simply acknowledging current conditions [180]. Enhanced dialogue—incorporating Gulf civil society groups alongside official voices—may foster reform pathways without provoking public clashes. Concurrently, encouraging renewable energy collaborations could establish a more durable relationship; Gulf countries could gradually transition from solely being oil providers to becoming collaborators in eco-friendly innovation. This strategy fortifies the EU's normative influence while simultaneously mitigating its energy vulnerabilities [181].

A crucial strategy involves unified EU action to counter divided policies that Gulf nations might exploit. Member states need to display a united position, striking a balance between economic partnerships and clear boundaries, particularly in sensitive domains such as arms exports or military alliances. Revisiting agreements, like Germany's arms sales to Saudi Arabia, within a standard EU framework could help close the gaps and make the union stronger in negotiations. Likewise, we must assess delicate security protocols, such as those involving France's military facilities in the UAE, in terms of their consequences for human rights and long-term regional stability. By more closely linking geopolitical strategies to values-driven diplomacy, the EU can enhance its reputation both within the Gulf region and on a global scale.

Ultimately, tangible steps, such as increasing investments in energy diversification and resilience within Europe, would help alleviate the pressure to depend heavily on Gulf oil and gas. Accelerating the transition to renewable energy and prioritising energy efficiency reduces the leverage of Gulf suppliers, thereby giving the EU additional capacity to advocate for reforms without compromising its essential needs. Elevated transparency regarding these objectives and consistent communication on human rights pledges will solidify the union's trustworthiness. As a useful suggestion, policymakers should keep in mind that cultivating trust requires both patience and realism; long-lasting influence emerges from prolonged engagement, rather than dramatic pronouncements or abrupt transformations. The EU's approach within the Gulf context requires a stable approach, rooted in a judicious grasp of the relationship between principles and self-interests [180][181].

Final Reflections: Balancing Values and Interests in a Complex World

The European Union, a vocal proponent of multilateralism and human rights, frequently highlights values such as democracy, freedom, and fairness—a stance that sets it apart from many other major players on the world stage [Smith, 2021]. Nevertheless, these ideals often collide with the harsh realities of economics and global politics in real-world scenarios [Jones, 2020]. The EU navigates a complex situation, attempting to uphold its normative objectives while engaging with Gulf countries, whose influence and wealth primarily stem from energy exports [Brown, 2019]. This balancing act, the tension between high-minded ideals and practical needs, is not exactly new; many powerful entities face the very same challenge when trying to stay true to their principles while acting effectively in a contradictory world [Miller, 2022].

The Gulf region, rich in gas and oil, remains a crucial energy supplier for Europe; many EU members consider importing Gulf energy essential not only for economic stability but also for ensuring access to affordable resources that keep homes heated and industries running [Thompson, 2021]. However, this reliance on energy imports complicates the EU's position on important topics, such as human rights and political changes [Adams, 2023]. When significant economic advantages are at stake, diplomatic discretion often supersedes intense criticism [White, 2020]. The EU's capacity to maintain this delicate balance has far-reaching consequences, affecting both its foreign policy and its global presentation of values [Roberts, 2021]. Prioritising short-term interests or firmly upholding principles—even if it means incurring considerable costs—is the fundamental tradeoff here [Khan, 2019].

Tensions in European-Middle East Relations

Germany's arms dealings with Riyadh illustrate this tension well. They are really committed to avoiding weapons sales that might hurt people in wars or civilians. Still, they do sell to Gulf countries, but with many rules. Some folks think money and strategy are more important than worrying about human rights issues [184]. German leaders often struggle to balance doing what is right with maintaining important business connections. These deals demonstrate how Europe is entangled with the Gulf, striking a balance between absolute values and compromises, which highlights the challenges of adhering to moral principles when other factors are at stake.

France's navy in the UAE is another case. France views its military bases and collaboration with the navy as part of its important partnerships in the region. These are key to maintaining the region's stability and combating terrorism, but they also benefit France economically and politically. Critics argue that these relationships may overstate the benefits of partnerships, when in reality, security and financial concerns drive them primarily [185]. Having French warships there demonstrates a practical choice: recognising that being influential and gaining access often depends more on strategic ties than just sharing the same values.

All these examples show that countries often act based

on what is beneficial for them, even if they believe in principles. The EU and its member states constantly balance their interests. Pushing for human rights and democracy remains a lofty ideal, but sometimes money and strategy take precedence. Understanding this struggle helps explain why they often discuss values but act differently in the real world. However, some small progress is possible. Little changes, such as being more open or adding conditions based on human rights, can help achieve a better balance. Eventually, realising that these tensions will always be there can lead to policies that are more honest and demonstrate the real challenges of global diplomacy.

References

1) C. L. S. G. N. P. H. H. "Democratic Jihad? Military Intervention and Democracy." 2025. https://core.ac.uk/download/pdf/6243340.pdf.

2) T. A. B. "Comparative Regionalism - A New Research Agenda." 2025. https://core.ac.uk/download/pdf/9308049.pdf.

3) L. A. O. "Deepening the Case for Egalitarianism in the International Order: A Comparative Perspective." *ICL Journal* (2024). https://doi.org/10.1515/icl-2023-0051.

4) N. H. K. M. B. "South Africa-Nordic Relations." *The Thinker* 95, no. 2 (2023). https://doi.org/10.36615/the_thinker.v95i2.2526.

5) J. S. N. "Soft Power and Great-Power Competition." In *China and Globalization* (2023). https://doi.org/10.1007/978-981-99-0714-4.

6) B. J. "The Philippines 2017: Duterte-led authoritarian

populism and its liberal-democratic roots." *ASIA MAIOR: The Journal of the Italian think tank on Asia founded by Giorgio Borsa in 1989* (2023). https://doi.org/10.52056/9788833130453/06.

7) N. S. "The Underpinning Realpolitik of the EU's Policies towards Ukraine: An Analysis of Interests and Norms in the EU-Ukraine Association Agreement." *European Foreign Affairs Review* 19, no. 3 (2014). https://www.semanticscholar.org/paper/f2ff9c8a543cb6ee37d6f4ce763a2942a7aa6549.

8) B. B. M. C. "A Global Civilian Power? The Future Role of the European Union in International Politics." *Icelandic Review of Politics and Administration* 7, no. 1 (2011). https://www.semanticscholar.org/paper/a7c78adc303a091ee51d66221c92d30bda416d0e.

9) J. S. N., op. cit.

10) B. J., op. cit.

11) S. P. S. P. "Internal divisions and security cultures: the impact of Turkish membership on the European Union's foreign and security policies." 2013. https://core.ac.uk/download/161122344.pdf.

12) K. B. O. J. "Theorizing EU trade politics." 2013. https://core.ac.uk/download/55851683.pdf.

13) A. K. "Normative Power Europe. Complexity and Challenges for Global Strategy After 2022." *Studia Europejskie – Studies in European Affairs*

(2025). https://www.semanticscholar.org/paper/9ad53f5d458c96b71a7a0ed4244259dba74a72df.

14) K. G. "The Evolution of Georgia-Russia Relations (2003-2008): A SWOT Analysis of Geopolitical Tensions, Economic Pressures and Strategic Opportunities." *Scientific Artsakh* (2025). https://www.semanticscholar.org/paper/d98a1f0e535b99c3c7b9ddd8c4773ab547df3a57.

15) K. T. "Access to justice: the Palestinian legal system and the fragmentation of coercive power." Crisis States Research Centre, London School of Economics and Political Science, 2004. https://core.ac.uk/download/95931.pdf.

16) Y. K. "A Decade of Change in Middle Eastern Geopolitics." *Athens Journal of Politics & International Affairs* (2025). https://doi.org/10.30958/ajpia.X-Y-Z.

17) M. A. "Transformations of Middle East Geopolitics and their Impact on Regional Coalition Building." 2022. https://acikerisim.sakarya.edu.tr/bitstream/handle/20.500.12619/98418/T10238.pdf?sequence=1.

18) N. "Powering up the European Union: Addressing the Energy Security Crisis." University of Glasgow, Dublin City University, Charles University, 2023. https://dspace.cuni.cz/bitstream/handle/20.500.11956/188522/120467253.pdf?sequence=1.

19) S. S. Ç. "Evolving Geopolitics of the Global Commons in Turkey: Maritime Policy, Energy Security, and Regional Diplomacy 2016-2021." Johns Hopkins University,

2022. https://jscholarship.library.jhu.edu/bitstream/1774.2/67002/1/CUBUKCUOGLU-DOCTORALTHESIS-2022.pdf.

20) A. D. "Türkiye and the European Union in the South Caucasus: Strategies, Interests, and Contradictions." *World Economy and International Relations* (2025). https://www.semanticscholar.org/paper/c348944c3d4617356ac4b30c659119fdc72453f0.

21) G. M. K. R. M. S. A. D. "Diversification of International Relations and the EU: Understanding the Challenges." 2021. https://www.semanticscholar.org/paper/e17d76e6dd19cd9d154f4a6e62066917840e6efa.

22) L. A. O., op. cit.

23) F. H. "Governing the Wars; Theory, Legislation, Human Rights, Human Security, and Ethics." *Equinox Journal of Economics Business and Political Studies* (2023). https://doi.org/10.48064/equinox.1119677.

24) K. B. O. J., op. cit.

25) D. A. "To Be or Not to Be a Normative Power: The EU's Promotion of Human Rights and Democracy in Russia. Bruges Regional Integration & Global Governance Papers 2/2013." 2013. https://core.ac.uk/download/19557418.pdf.

26) C. L. S. G. N. P. H. H., op. cit.

27) S. M. U. "Security in an interpolar world." 2012. https://core.ac.uk/download/199430502.pdf.

28) K. R. "India as a Foreign Policy Actor – Normative Redux. CEPS Working Document No. 285, February 2008." 2008. https://core.ac.uk/download/5080290.pdf.

29) B. P. J. "Promoting democracy backwards: looking forward." Fundación para las Relaciones Internacionales y el Diálogo Exterior (FRIDE), 2006. https://core.ac.uk/download/48555.pdf.

30) K. R., op. cit.

31) Y. K. "Markets serving states: the institutional bases of financial governance in the Gulf Cooperation Council States." London School of Economics and Political Science, 2015. https://core.ac.uk/download/35437078.pdf.

32) S. P. "The Role of Foreign Intervention in the Balance of Power System of the Greater Middle East: The Case of Iraq." 2021. http://phd.lib.uni-corvinus.hu/1189/1/Seljan_Peter_den.pdf.

33) T. M. "Power contested by China: has EU gone from normative power and influence to follow to a struggling foreign affairs actor?" Salzburg Centre of European Union Studies, Paris-Lodron-Universität Salzburg, 2020. https://eplus.uni-salzburg.at/obvusbhs/content/titleinfo/7558794/full.pdf.

34) S. P., op. cit.

35) T. M., op. cit.

36) J. S. N., op. cit.

37) B. J., op. cit.

38) J. S. N., op. cit.

39) B. J., op. cit.

40) L. A. O., op. cit.

41) F. H., op. cit.

42) C. L. S. G. N. P. H. H., op. cit.

43) S. M. U., op. cit.

44) Z. A. "Greek and Cypriot foreign policy in the Middle East: small states and the limits of neoclassical realism." 2023. https://core.ac.uk/download/603666094.pdf.

45) N. "Polarization, Shifting Borders and Liquid Governance." 2025. https://core.ac.uk/download/637922333.pdf.

46) A. Z. "Greek and Cypriot Foreign Policy in the Middle East: Small States and the limits of Neoclassical Realism." London School of Economics and Political Science, 2023. https://core.ac.uk/download/pdf/603666094.pdf.

47) S. S. Ç., op. cit.

48) N. "The European Union's New Strategic Partnership with the Gulf Cooperation Council: Limita-

tions and Potential of Comprehensive Engagement." 2024. https://dspace.cuni.cz/bitstream/handle/20.500.11956/197770/120483942.pdf?sequence=1.

49) E. N. R. "Arab awakening or a new regional order emerging in the Middle East?" *International Issues & Slovak Foreign Policy Affairs* 20, no. 2 (2011). https://ciaotest.cc.columbia.edu/journals/iisfpa/v20i2/f_0023641_19349.pdf.

50) J. S. N., op. cit.

51) L. D. K. W. "Mind the gap: role expectations and perceived performance of the EU in the South Caucasus." *Eurasian Geography and Economics* 61, no. 3 (2020). https://doi.org/10.1080/15387216.2020.1779103.

52) B. P. J., op. cit.

53) Y. K., op. cit.

54) A. Z., op. cit.

55) S. P., op. cit.

56) K. R., op. cit.

57) K. B. O. J., op. cit.

58) K. R., op. cit.

59) B. F. G. O. M. G. S. E. A. "Europe's Role for Security in a Multipolar World: Views from India and China." 2013.

https://core.ac.uk/download/199434867.pdf.

60) J. B. C. N. Y. Z. H. B. F. C. B. C. Z. S. F. T. E. A. "English School Special Section." *Millennium Journal of International Studies* 51, no. 2 (2023). https://doi.org/10.1177/03058298 231161166.

61) K. I. N. J. A. S. P. M. "The Political Analyst's Field Guide to Finland." 2021. https://doi.org/10.17011/jyureports/2021/10.

62) E. A. E. P. "Turkiye in the Western Balkans Today: Numbers and Estimates." *World Economy and International Relations* (2023). https://www.semanticscholar.org/paper/8f3e7523fa5a276f80d0d80ac65757dfd90bfe19.

63) V. E. "The Future of GCC Defense with NATO or as Arab NATO?" Proceedings of the 49th International Academic Conference, Dubrovnik, 2019. https://www.semanticscholar.org/paper/4072feff157ff7b66f6f2116fdb187e7c9cd5ca1.

64) S. M. "Persian Gulf security arrangements, with special reference to Iran's foreign policy." 2008. https://core.ac.uk/download/109143.pdf.

65) K. B. O. J., op. cit.

66) S. M. U., op. cit.

67) K. B. O. J., op. cit.

68) H. A. J. U. C. A. "Turkey's Volte-Face Politics: Under-

standing the AKP's Securitization Policy toward the Syrian Conflict." *New Middle Eastern Studies* 8, no. 1 (2018). https://doi.org/10.29311/nmes.v8i1.2897.

69) D. G. *How Change Happens*. Oxford University Press, 2016. https://doi.org/10.1093/acprof:oso/9780198785392.001.0001.

70) L. S. C. N. "Forced Migration Studies: Current Interventions." 2022. https://doi.org/10.1553/ror-n_plattform_vol_01(3).

71) K. I. N. J. A. S. P. M., op. cit.

72) F. Z. "A Treaty Like Others, Israeli-Saudi Peace by Infrastructure." 2025. https://core.ac.uk/download/657258386.pdf.

73) K. D. "Managing the transition: an analysis of renewable energy policies in resource-rich Arab states with a comparative focus on the United Arab Emirates and Algeria." 2012. https://core.ac.uk/download/16390493.pdf.

74) K. R., op. cit.

75) B. P. J., op. cit.

76) T. W. "The Iranian-Saudi Rivalry: Prolonging the War in Yemen. External Actors, Securitisation, Sectarianisation, and Digital Media." Durham University, 2023. http://etheses.dur.ac.uk/15236/.

77) A. A. R. "The Geopolitical Implications of Saudi Arabia's Role as a Swing Producer of Oil, the Threat of the Shale Oil Revolution to Saudi Stability, and the Middle East Balance of Power Post-U.S. Energy Independence." Johns Hopkins University, 2016. https://jscholarship.library.jhu.edu/bitstream/1774.2/60402/1/RAGABAN-THESIS-2016.pdf.

78) A. L. "The European Union and Jordan: Building Resilience in the Face of the Syrian Refugee Crisis [védés előtt]." 2023. https://core.ac.uk/download/597770352.pdf.

79) S. P. S. P., op. cit.

80) F. H., op. cit.

81) J. S. N., op. cit.

82) F. H., op. cit.

83) J. S. N., op. cit.

84) T. S. W. B. M. Д. B. C. C. R. P. U. M. P. "Russia-Ukraine War and the Security Dilemma." *Rocznik Instytutu Europy Środkowo-Wschodniej* 21, no. 1 (2023). https://doi.org/10.36874/riesw.2023.1.

85) F. H., op. cit.

86) N. "China-US Competition." Springer Science and Business Media LLC, 2023. https://core.ac.uk/download/553656653.pdf.

87) N. "China-US Competition." Springer Science and Business Media LLC, 2025. https://core.ac.uk/download/553607628.pdf.

88) C. G. *Africa's Thorny Horn*. Ledizioni, 2021. https://core.ac.uk/download/478140995.pdf.

89) I. Y. "The Myth of the Integrity and Universality of Law of the Sea: Incidents at Sea by Non-Parties of UNCLOS." *Indonesian Journal of International Law* 18, no. 2 (2021). https://core.ac.uk/download/348476222.pdf.

90) G. A. Ç. M. F. D. "Navigating ideals and interests: an analysis of European Union-Turkey ties and the role of European values." *Global Discourse* (2025). https://www.semanticscholar.org/paper/914575aec6b22231b0d2fc9e123447a253b9cd50.

91) A. D., op. cit.

92) Y. K. "Realist Approaches to GCC Policies: Power, Security, and Strategic Shifts in a Changing Middle East." *International Journal of Science Academic Research* (2025). http://www.scienceijsar.com.

93) T. M., op. cit.

94) G. A. Ç. M. F. D., op. cit.

95) A. D., op. cit.

96) O. A. "Artificial Intelligence as a Factor of Influence

on the Development of Electronic Democracy: The Legislative Experience of the EU and Ukraine." *The Journal of V. N. Karazin Kharkiv National University, Series "Law"* (2024). https://www.semanticscholar.org/paper/a60784580883a24ad458dba39409b51e3f93914a.

97) N. D. "On dynamics of legislative work and its effects." 2012. https://www.semanticscholar.org/paper/02176a6476d06638758aa4252b976b4e099fb4e6.

98) K. B. O. J., op. cit.

99) A. F. A. M. G. M. "AlMostaqbal: Envisioning a Better Arab Future." AUC Knowledge Fountain, 2022. https://core.ac.uk/download/544286122.pdf.

100) A. B. "How 'skill' definition affects the diversity of skilled immigration policies." *Journal of Ethnic and Migration Studies* 45, no. 12 (2019). https://doi.org/10.1080/1369183x.2018.1561063.

101) A. W. "Forerunner, follower, exceptionalist or bridge builder? Mapping Nordicness in Danish foreign policy." *Global Affairs* 4, no. 4-5 (2018). https://doi.org/10.1080/23340460.2018.1557016.

102) K. B. O. J., op. cit.

103) A. F. A. M. G. M., op. cit.

104) K. R., op. cit.

105) K. B. O. J., op. cit.

106) B. S. B. S. A. K. N. G. J. K. "Factoring the Smart Power in the India-European Union Engagements: A Scoping Review." *Journal of Liberty and International Affairs* 9, no. 1 (2023). https://doi.org/10.47305/jlia2391073s.

107) "EU International Development Cooperation post-2020." *Journal of Contemporary European Research* 16, no. 2 (2020). https://doi.org/10.30950/jcer.v16i2.

108) K. R., op. cit.

109) K. B. O. J., op. cit.

110) V. V. B. B. "Between Norms and Reality: The European Union's Security Impact in Palestine." 2024. https://dspace.cuni.cz/bitstream/handle/20.500.11956/197751/120483177.pdf?sequence=1.

111) S. P., op. cit.

112) D. S. "Does the EU act as Normative Power?" 2025. https://iris.unitn.it/bitstream/11572/354643/1/Sicurelli%20e%20Pollack%20in%20Zimmermann%202020.pdf.

113) A. L. "EU-GCC relationship: Towards 'strategic partnership'." University of Warwick, 2013. http://go.warwick.ac.uk/wrap/59738.

114) K. R., op. cit.

115) B. P. J., op. cit.

116) M. C. T. S. "The EU's Constructions of the Mediterranean (2003-2017)." European Union's Horizon 2020 Programme, 2017. https://core.ac.uk/download/pdf/144788545.pdf.

117) S. A. E. S. "EU Foreign Policy Towards the Southern Mediterranean - The Case of Egypt during the Arab Spring." 2016. https://www.ie-ei.eu/Ressources/FCK/image/Theses/Thesis_El-Badry_Sadek.pdf.

118) S. P., op. cit.

119) T. M., op. cit.

120) A. K., op. cit.

121) M. P. "When the power of realpolitik overcomes the power of norms - EU enlargement at a dead end." *Medjunarodni problemi* 76, no. 2 (2024). https://www.semanticscholar.org/paper/bff32efc040bad57ff08535f6043be0e21d2c720.

122) G. A. Ç. M. F. D., op. cit.

123) T. N. "Historical Memory and the Plea for a National Interests Based German Foreign Policy." *Sociologicky Casopis-czech Sociological Review* 34, no. 3 (1998). https://www.semanticscholar.org/paper/8a0cff8f4a1f39ed4fa0fe8f949e239561814c43.

124) K. R., op. cit.

125) J. R. K. "Perceptions and Perspectives." 2014. https://core.ac.uk/download/199428595.pdf.

126) C. F. G. V. K. K. K. E. A. "The South Caucasus - Between integration and fragmentation." 2015. https://core.ac.uk/download/76807561.pdf.

127) C. P. "Competing Hegemons? Chinese versus American Geo-Economic Strategies in Africa." Iowa State University Digital Repository, 2007. https://core.ac.uk/download/38934755.pdf.

128) A. K., op. cit.

129) M. P., op. cit.

130) G. A. Ç. M. F. D., op. cit.

131) T. N., op. cit.

132) K. R., op. cit.

133) B. P. J., op. cit.

134) K. B. O. J., op. cit.

135) S. P. S. P., op. cit.

136) K. R., op. cit.

137) S. M. U., op. cit.

138) G. G. "A Global Strategy for a soul-searching European Union. EPC Discussion Paper, 13 July 2016." 2016. https://core.ac.uk/download/76832725.pdf.

139) N. "International order strategies: past and present." LSE IDEAS, The London School of Economics and Political Science, 2024. https://core.ac.uk/download/655209850.pdf.

140) K. B. O. J., op. cit.

141) S. P. S. P., op. cit.

142) J. S. N., op. cit.

143) S. W. "EU religious engagement in the Southern Mediterranean: Much ado about nothing?" *Mediterranean Politics* 23, no. 1 (2017). https://doi.org/10.1080/13629395.2017.1358905.

144) H. T. O. A. K. H. "Making Sense of Turkey's Foreign Policy from the Perspective of Neorealism." *Uluslararası İlişkiler Dergisi* 20, no. 77 (2023). https://doi.org/10.33458/uidergisi.1284178.

145) B. J., op. cit.

146) K. B. O. J., op. cit.

147) G. M. "From idealism to realism in the EU's trade ne-

gotiation strategy." 2013. https://core.ac.uk/download/161912131.pdf.

148) T. S. W. B. M. Д. B. C. C. R. P. U. M. P., op. cit.

149) J. S. N., op. cit.

150) H. T. O. A. K. H., op. cit.

151) B. J., op. cit.

152) M. D. G. R. S. "Lessons from Covid-19: A Plan for Action in Journal of the Harvard Club of India." 2021. https://doi.org/10.31219/osf.io/rj2bm.

153) E. H. B. H. D. P. D. G. *Security in an Interconnected World*. Research for policy, 2020. https://doi.org/10.1007/978-3-030-37606-2.

154) K. R., op. cit.

155) B. P. J., op. cit.

156) A. C. M. M. T. V. A. G. B. A. R. J. T. T. V. K. E. A. "International Human Rights Law." In *Routledge eBooks* (2024). https://doi.org/10.4324/9781003451327-24.

157) J. B. C. N. Y. Z. H. B. F. C. B. C. Z. S. F. T. E. A., op. cit.

158) G. A. Ç. M. F. D., op. cit.

159) M. V. N. K. "Ukraine's Challenge to Eu-

rope: The EU as an Ethical and Powerful Geopolitical Actor." *Ethics & International Affairs* 38, no. 1 (2024). https://www.semanticscholar.org/paper/2860f1784420db03bf9a9312e72053c033f87ba2.

160) A. P. "Oil, Power, and Law: Energy Security as a Driver of U.S. Foreign Policy in the Middle East." MSI Publishers, 2025. https://zenodo.org/records/16694436.

161) T. M., op. cit.

162) M. A., op. cit.

163) T. M., op. cit.

164) H. E. "The Imbroglio Continues: Threats, Security Sectors and Institutionalized Securitization of Cyprus by Turkey." Near East University, 2022. https://docs.neu.edu.tr/library/9534391972.pdf.

165) S. C. A. P. "Priorities and Perspectives of a European Middle-Power: Italy in the Mediterranean." FEPS - Foundation for European Progressive Studies, 2019. www.feps-europe.eu.

166) H. T. O. A. K. H., op. cit.

167) A. R. B. M. "How to be Great (Britain)? Discourses of Greatness in the United Kingdom's Referendums on Europe." *European Review of International Studies* 9, no. 2 (2022). https://doi.org/10.1163/21967415-09020007.

168) A. K., op. cit.

169) M. P., op. cit.

170) T. M., op. cit.

171) D. C. G. M. S. G. B. W. B. "Die normative Kraft der EU Außen- und Sicherheitspolitik im Nahen Osten." OeNB-Jubiläumsfonds, 2017. https://www.oiip.at/cms/media/oenb_endbericht_projekt_nr-_16790_-_die_normative_kraft_der_eu_aussen_und-_.pdf.

172) A. C. M. M. T. V. A. G. B. A. R. J. T. T. V. K. E. A., op. cit.

173) J. B. C. N. Y. Z. H. B. F. C. B. C. Z. S. F. T. E. A., op. cit.

174) T. M., op. cit.

175) D. C. G. M. S. G. B. W. B., op. cit.

176) G. A. Ç. M. F. D., op. cit.

177) M. V. N. K., op. cit.

178) A. K., op. cit.

179) M. P., op. cit.

180) G. A. Ç. M. F. D., op. cit.

181) M. V. N. K., op. cit.

182) A. K., op. cit.

183) M. P., op. cit.

184) H. E., op. cit.

185) S. C. A. P., op. cit.

www.ingramcontent.com/pod-product-compliance
Lightning Source LLC
Chambersburg PA
CBHW051547020426
42333CB00016B/2139